Curiosity Killed the Hedonist

20 Sarcastic Adventure Stories Which Give a Glimpse of Life on the Wrong Side of the Global Railroad Tracks

Gregory D.B. Holt

ISBN: 1468118870
ISBN-13: 978-1468118872

DEDICATION

Dedicated to my amazing nieces and nephew:
Margaret, Ava, Vivian, Victoria, and Taylor

CONTENTS

DISCLAIMER

"The following is a true story; only the names have been changed … to protect the guilty."

Lyrics from *Ain't No Fun Waitin' Round to be a Millionaire,*

Bonn Scott, AC/DC, 1976

1 RUSSIA: A TRANS-SIBERIAN MISADVENTURE

I was trolling for chicks in Lenin Square. It was a routine evening in the industrial city of Novosibirsk, Siberia, Russia. As any seasoned traveller of the former Soviet Union knows, all real cities have a statue of Lenin and a giant T-34 tank which commemorates The Great Patriotic War (known in some countries as World War II). The best way to meet girls in countries like Russia, Ukraine, Kazakhstan, and Belarus is to go to the statue of Lenin and ask for directions from Lenin to the T-34 tank. This often leads to an interesting conversation about Russian pop music, the different ways to make borsch soup, or a deep analysis of the girl's thesis in nuclear physics. If you strike out, you go to the T-34 and ask for directions back to the statue of Lenin.

That night, unfortunately, Lenin was unattended by his usual entourage of good-looking citizens. So I decided to head for the airport to begin my adventure. I was to fly to Moscow, do some sightseeing, then return to Siberia across the great Russian steppe by train. I would be fulfilling every train fanatic's deepest desire: to ride on the Trans-Siberian Railway. The whole route takes 5 days; my little piece of it would be a mere 50 hours.

I walked up a street looking for a taxi to go to the airport. Out of nowhere, about 5 guys showed up wearing Adidas track suits and Charles Dickens artful dodger caps. One guy started punching me in the eye, one was hitting me in the back of the head, one was jabbing me in the ribs from the side, and another was stomping on my ankle. Advice givers like to offer after the fact suggestions such as, "Why didn't you say 'hey fellas, how about you take all the cash in my wallet for free and let me go on my merry way?'" But everything happened in a split second and it actually took several punches in my eye for me to realize that I was getting my ass kicked.

After belatedly clueing in to my unfortunate situation, I launched three vicious elbow strikes right into the first guy's mouth. I could feel his face cracking and I'm pretty sure I knocked one of his teeth out. He ran off, and his buddies followed him. But without my even feeling it, they had snatched my wallet. Not to mention, they had thoroughly beaten the crap out of me.

After my adrenaline died down, I realized was unable to stand up straight and I did the old sit down and tumble over onto the pavement maneuver. I sat stunned for a while, and then realized that I was cold as hell and had a plane to catch. I did a quick inventory check: passport, cell phone, bag, and watch, were all intact. I also had a secret stash of about $180 in my bag.

At this point, I had to make a quick decision: fly to one of the world's most expensive cities with no credit cards and only a handful of cash? Or, return to my cozy, warm apartment in Novosibirsk where I had friends, food, and my favorite pillow? The latter option was more sensible, but I despised the notion that those 5 assholes could ruin my Trans-Siberian rail adventure. So I flagged a cab to the airport and headed for Russia's mega-city.

Moscow was rough. I was close to broke, I had bruises all over my body, and I was limping because the guy who had been kicking my ankle had done a proper job of it. I paid 14 precious rubles (50 cents) to use a public bathroom, and when I looked in the mirror I saw a horrifying gigantic black, red, blue, and purple eye looking back at me. It begged the question, why do they call it a black eye when there are so many other colors to choose from? I found out later, much to my delight, that Russians call it a blue eye.

Moscow prices are out of this world and I quickly realized that things like restaurants, hotels, and museums were way out of my budget. I bought a 2-liter bottle of water and a big loaf of bread, and proceeded to limp around the city looking at Moscow's grand symbols such as Red Square, St. Basil's Cathedral, and the Kremlin. The city was really alive, and the mere pulse of Russia's vibrant capital kept me going. I felt I had seen at least half of Moscow's major attractions from the outside. After a day and night of sightseeing I was ready to head home to Siberia. I briefly considered following my Siberian friend's advice: "Greg, man, when you go to Moscow, stay all night at the discotecas to keep warm, then sleep in the churches by day." But I didn't want to risk not being able to afford a train ticket back.

The train station in Moscow was a challenge. The line for tickets was painfully long, and everybody was yelling and shoving to get a few seconds with the crabby old bitch behind the counter who yells at you then sells you a ticket. One guy, about 45 years old, pushed his way to the front of the line. He was the quintessential fat, muscular, slightly balding, sort of drunk, Russian guy. Two small women, about 25, objected to his cutting the line. He waved his hairy forearm at them threateningly and yelled at them in a vicious, deep, voice. Then a 25 year old Russian guy stepped in on behalf of the girls. The hairy forearms started waving wildly, tempers soared, and the two men squared off. Both men raised their fists in a technically correct boxing stance. The middle aged guy kept yelling loudly, swung his fists and missed the young guy by a mile. Then the young guy landed two perfect jabs down the middle, and a right hook to the face which sent the guy flying back on his ass. He sat on his but for about half a second, dabbed his nose with his hand, and found that he had blood all over his face. He gave a shrug of his shoulders and a look that seemed to say "No big deal," then jumped right back up and started yelling in the face of the young man again. The two argued for a while then seemed to say, "Let's continue this later outside, but first buy our tickets so we don't lose our place in line."

Eventually I got my turn at the front of the line and was shocked to hear that the train to Novosibirsk cost $200, which was more than I had. I wandered aimlessly in the station a bit and tried to decide what to do. I looked up in my Russian dictionary all the words I could find for "second class," "cheap," and "dirt cheap". I settled on the word "PlatzKart" which means proletariat class on a Russian train. I went through the human obstacle course to get to the front of the line again. This time I used the word "PlatzKart" and somehow explained to the lady that I was down to 3,900 Rubles (about $130). She looked something up, shook her head, and said in Russian "No places!" I asked, "Later train?" in Russian, and after some fiddling she found me a ticket for 3,000 Rubles. It was PlatzKart and it left from a station somewhere else in Moscow at 3 a.m. I bought it.

I hobbled through Moscow's Metro system to get to the other train station, and then killed 6 hours watching Muscovites drift in and out of the station. Fortunately, the train station had a café which made a cheap and tasty bowl of borsch. I took two.

PlatzKart is basically a bunch of bunk beds stacked up in the train, without compartments or privacy. (Think train for retreating German soldiers in a World War II movie). But I was so cold and tired by the time my train lumbered in that my little upper bunk space on the train felt like a 5-star luxury suite. There was a chubby, old, smiling woman who was in charge of the car. She brought everyone sheets, a blanket, and a pillow. She also delivered tea, coffee, and snacks for a small price. I had a safe place to sleep, food, a giant Tolstoy novel, and 50 hours to heal on the rails.

After a great night's sleep, I awoke to the chatter of Uzbeks, Belarusians, Ukrainians, and Russians all making their way East from Moscow across the vast expanse of Russia. An old babushka with a scarf wrapped around her head came waddling down the corridor. When she saw me her eyes lit up, and she gave a giant, toothless smile. She grabbed my arm, pointed at my blue eye and said, "Oyyyy! Kak Krasivy!" (How handsome!) A bunch of other passengers saw this and chuckled. Then they all proceeded to ask me what happened.

As I told the story people seemed to wander over from the other bunk beds to hover and listen. Using broken Russian and lots of hand gestures I described my night in Novosibirsk. One crusty old timer said, "Ha! I bet that guy is using your money to buy a new gold tooth!" A woman asked if I went to the police. The old guy laughed loudly and said, "The police! They wouldn't do anything except take more of your money!"

A group of 4 young Belarusian guys from Minsk patted me on the back and expressed admiration for what they saw as a badge of honor. I asked them about Belarus, and they said, "It is a clean, beautiful country. We have a good, strong dictator." They gave me some Belarusian money which they said was worthless. A Ukrainian man listening to the story said, "Siberia is crazy," and he gave me a big lump of fat wrapped in newspaper. This was sala, a tasty Ukrainian delicacy.

Later that night, I was talking to a middle-aged guy who could have been the twin brother of the hairy bastard from the train station. He sold electric railway poles for a living. We went down to the dining car and ate some dinner. The old woman running the dining car was very friendly and she sat at our table and talked with us. At the table next to us was yet another middle-aged, hairy, muscular, fat man. He was doing vodka shots with one of the waitresses, a young woman in tight pants whose work on the train seemed to have given her an extra 80 pounds. Another heavy-set waitress with partially exposed cleavage showed up and joined the vodka shots table.

Suddenly, the older woman turned off the lights, turned them back on again, and kicked me and most of the other diners out of the dining car. It was rather abrupt and I hadn't really finished off my dinner. The guy I had been talking to walked back to our car excitedly, dug something out of his bag, laughed sheepishly, and told me he was going back to the dining car. "But they're closed," I said.

"No," he said, "Now it's time for doing the sex with those girls." I was shocked.

"You mean those girls are prostitutes?" I asked.

"No," he replied, "they are waitresses. But if you pay them you can do the sex!" And he laughed again and hurried off to the dining car/brothel. I retired to my bunk bed and read a chapter of Tolstoy which happened to be about a Russian aristocrat having a decadent meal, doing vodka shots, and then going to a brothel.

Early the next morning, I woke up and noticed the train had stopped at a small city in the middle of nowhere. The electric pole salesman was drinking beer for breakfast and admiring the view. I walked down the corridor to ask for some tea. Suddenly, 8 policemen in commando-style uniforms sealed off each end of the train car and boarded the train. Their lead man noticed me, pointed at me and rushed up to me. "Document!" he yelled. I gave him my passport. He laughed and said to his team in Russian,

"Not him." Then they moved rapidly passed me. Seconds later, they were dragging some guy off the train in handcuffs. My tea arrived, and the train pulled out.

Eventually, my 50-hour fun pass on the Trans-Siberian Railway expired and the train arrived in Novosibirsk. I limped off the train and made my way down to Lenin Square where I could catch a bus home. But before getting on the bus I noticed two hotskies in mini-skirts smoking cigarettes on a bench near Lenin. I thought about going to talk to them. I hadn't showered in days, I was unshaven, I smelled like PlatzKart, I had a limp, and an ugly blue eye. But what the hell; I went over to the girls and asked for directions to the T-34 tank…

2 EGYPT: THE BATTLE OF THE NILE

Cairo was too quiet. It was the morning of Friday, January 28th, 2011. Most of the city's 18 Million residents were listening to the mosque sermons and calls to prayer which echoed all across the vast landscape of dirty, 20-story buildings, medieval forts, stunning mosques, and ancient pyramids. When Friday prayers end, there is usually a return to the continuous urban chorus of honking horns, bargaining leather jacket salesmen, and chatty Egyptians drinking Turkish coffee. But today there was only silence and an aura of anticipation.

Over the last few days demonstrators had taken to the streets and called for the resignation of President Hosni Mubarak. I saw about 5,000 people cross the Nile River from West to East into Tahrir Square, which is in downtown Cairo. Thousands of riot police deployed and used tear gas, billy clubs, shields, and riot trucks, to disperse the crowds which began to pop up all over downtown Cairo. My Egyptian friends described these police as the loyal attack dogs of Mubarak's regime. Some of these guys started working around police stations at the age of 13. They were gradually raised by the wider police family to become enforcers of the martial law which Mubarak declared in Egypt 31 years ago when Anwar Sadat was assassinated and Mubarak was promoted from Vice President to President. I had been hit by small amounts of tear gas launched by these police, a friend in my hostel had been clubbed in the back by plain clothes cops who were using sticks to spread panic ahead of the riot trucks, and another friend had been robbed by a group of five men who had a gun and police I.D.'s. Most of the demonstrators I saw during this period looked afraid and tended to retreat when riot control lines marched down the streets. An odd exception was the steps of the National Press Club where a few hundred demonstrators listened to a speech given by a young woman while right next to them about 200 riot police waited silently and sealed off the street.

The first few days of the demonstration were effectively controlled or disrupted by the police. Internet and cell phones were shut down across Egypt by the Government, few working-class Egyptians could afford to risk leaving their jobs in already dire economic circumstances, and there must have been a reluctance to believe all this was really happening since there had been nothing like it in the 31 years of Mubarak's rule. Thus, as of early Friday morning, the riot police were firmly in control.

But Friday is the Muslim holy day, and a day off work for most Egyptians. By now, word of mouth had spread through Egypt that today was going to be the big day. Demonstrators had learned to bring masks and bandanas to combat the effects of tear gas and they were more accustomed to the fear tactics of the riot police.

Personally, I had no desire to get caught up in someone else's political turmoil, so I paid my way onto the pool deck of the Grand Hyatt Hotel which had a great view of the Nile River Bridges, and an efficient poolside beverage service. The best place to watch a revolution is from a hot tub, and since it was a perfect day I was also able to work on my tan.

"Pop! Pop! Pop!" There was a continuous popping sound similar to that made by those idiotic T-shirt cannons which third rate sports arenas use to keep fans awake. I saw tear gas shells launched in a long arc from the El Galaa Bridge into El Galaa Square. It was a continuous firing process which resulted in a large, thick, tear gas cloud hovering in El Galaa Square. Without a gas mask, it would have been near impossible to run through the cloud, and anyone making it through the cloud would be met by about 600 riot police formed up in a tight blocking position which sealed off the western entrance of El Galaa Bridge. In addition, there were police boats guarding against amphibious crossings.

The crowd was assembling near a building which housed Mohamed El Barradi, the Nobel Prize winning physicist who many considered to be an opposition leader. They apparently wanted to cross over the Nile bridges and into Tahrir Square as they had done on Tuesday. But this time their route was firmly blocked by the riot police. In addition to the defenses described above, the police had hundreds more men in reserve in Tahrir Square, as well as water cannons mounted on vehicles. Earlier in the morning, on my way to the Hyatt, I saw many of these police forming up. In spite of their youth, they looked focused, prepared, and determined. Their older leaders were actively trooping their lines and getting them geared up for the day's events. At that point, I would have bet money that not a single demonstrator would be able to cross from West of the Nile into Downtown Cairo.

But I had underestimated both the size and determination of the crowd. Little by little, the crowd started to creep into the edges of El Galaa Square, chanting loudly and shaking their fists. Individual demonstrators would bravely charge towards the police, throw a rock, then run back, coughing up tear gas. The crowd continued to edge further into the Square, and as they did so the police doubled down on the tear gas firing. A nearby apartment caught fire somehow. Soon a fire engine came to extinguish it while both the police and the demonstrators allowed it through. The crowd kept getting braver, occasionally rushing right to the bridge in groups of 20 or 30, only to be beaten back. This continued for about an hour and the demonstrators had made no progress towards penetrating the bridge. Police reinforcements began to arrive as it became clear that El Galaa Bridge was the decisive point in their attempt to keep the demonstrators out of downtown. The rushes of the crowd got even bigger and more determined, but still the police beat them back and continued to rain tear gas on the square with deadly accuracy.

Demonstrators grabbed some tear gas bombs which had landed, ran towards the police, and chucked them onto the bridge. This caused a bit of wavering in the police lines, but not enough to shake them. In spite of their lack of success so far, the crowd continued to surge toward the police. The stinging of the tear gas must have been intense at this point, but a small group got close to the bridge for long enough to start a large fire. Thick black smoke enveloped the police, and the crowd spontaneously surged toward the bridge. This was the critical point in the battle where the police finally broke ranks and began to retreat. After falling back a few hundred meters, the police recovered and reformed into another choke point on the east edge of El Galaa Bridge, just before Zamalek Island. But at that point, their tear gas shots were landing in the Nile River, unable to hit the relatively thin target of the bridge. On the rare shots when gas did hit the bridge, demonstrators would grab the canister and either toss it into The Nile or back at the police.

A ripple of enthusiasm went through the crowd as they realized that the police choke point on the bridge had been broken. Thousands of demonstrators filled into El Galaa Square and onto the bridge. Many more were behind them but still out of view. The police were vulnerable and the crowd knew it.

The riot police held out at their new choke point for about 30 minutes, and then they retreated to the Qasr el-Nil Bridge which connects Zamalek Island to Central Cairo. This gave them the opportunity to use the traffic circle in front of the Cairo Opera House as another tear gas choke point, backed up by police in reserve on Qasr el-Nil Bridge. This obstacle also proved formidable, but after about an hour of repeating the tactics of charging, throwing rocks, setting fires, and then surging in as a group, the demonstrators again broke through.

My heart sank as the violence approached The Cairo Opera House. I had recently seen Giuseppe Verde's opera "Aida" there. It had been a beautiful night. Our dates were gorgeous Danish-Jordanian girls and the opera, set in ancient Egypt, had a tragic but romantic ending. Unlike many Western countries where it it's considered un-cool to dress up for opera and theater, Egypt is stylishly formal and refuses entry to inappropriately dressed scruff. So my friend and I wore sharp suits, the girls wore delicious, dark, evening gowns, and one of the girls even had a lovely white flower pinned in her hair. After the opera, we journeyed up Zamalek Island to a traditional restaurant which used recipes from the secret cookbook of an Egyptian who was once the personal chef of the Ottoman Sultan. We ate baba ganoush and kafta, smoked shisha, drank Egyptian tea, and the girls taught us a few rare Arabic expressions. Nights like these are common in romantic Cairo, and in the absence of revolution, the streets fill up every night with Egyptian culture and smiling Cairoenes.

But Aida's romantic theme would take a back seat this week to two other themes which are strong in that opera: respect for the Egyptian Army, and the everlasting nature of authoritarian governments in Egypt. Many people had had enough of the current authoritarian government, and right in front of the opera they were attacking one manifestation of that government, the riot police. (In contrast to the riot police, most Egyptians have a profound respect for their Army, and this would be an important factor in the days to come).

The demonstrators forced their way onto Qasr el-Nil Bridge and this time the retreat of the police seemed a bit more rushed. Once again, the tear gas was rendered ineffective since the bridge was too narrow to hit consistently with long range tear gas shots. The demonstrators pushed the police all the way to the East edge of the Nile, and it looked as if they would break into Tahrir Square.

This is when the police unleashed their water cannons along with a detachment of reserve troops. The fire hose strength spray of the cannons drove the crowd back and then fresh troops rushed in to shove and sweep the demonstrators along the bridge. This was very effective and the crowd was pushed back to the beautiful Opera House. Tear gas shots once again arced into the crowd. Another stalemate ensued near the opera for about 30 minutes. Over the next hour the crowd was swept all the way back to the El Galaa Bridge.

Now imagine the state of exhaustion of the demonstrators after 3 or 4 hours of running, shoving, jumping around, and dodging tear gas, clubs and water cannons. Not to mention, they had just lost almost all of the ground they had gained which must have been demoralizing. But the riot police were also exhausted, and more demonstrators piled in from El Galaa Square.

At this point, perhaps 10,000 demonstrators were trying to push across the El Galaa Bridge against now sluggish resistance by the police. The two groups resembled two heavy weight boxers in the later rounds of a fight who just embrace and shove each other around because they are too tired to swing. But the demonstrators still had enough fight left to slog the riot police back to the opera, and then all the way to the end of the Qasr el-Nil Bridge. After about 4 or 5 hours of struggle, the demonstrators had successfully crossed the Nile.

"Sir would you care for another tonic water, or perhaps some Turkish coffee?" asked the pool waiter. I declined and he proceeded to tell me about a nationwide 6 p.m. curfew which meant the Hyatt was not letting anybody out of its doors after 6. It was now 5:50 p.m. They offered to arrange a room for me, but I wasn't sure if that meant a free sympathy room or a full priced room. The Grand Hyatt was one of the nicest and most expensive places in town, and I was too broke to risk paying for a night there when I already had a perfectly decent $14/night hostel in downtown Cairo. I got dressed, guzzled as much free Hyatt water as I could, and then made for the exit.

Within minutes I was on the streets just South of Tahrir Square trying to work my way to my hostel which was up north by Talat Harb Square. Every street I tried to use was flooded by people rushing south, coughing up tear gas, and telling me the route was closed or too dangerous. It was dark now, I was alone, cell phones were cut off, and the streets of Cairo were erupting. Catching a taxi was not an option. The few that were still running were packed with fleeing families. Transportation away from downtown was in such short supply that when a donkey pulling a vegetable cart stopped, 10 people jumped on it for a ride.

Luckily I had my trusty map, and I decided to follow the Nile River south towards Maadi, a relatively wealthy and hopefully safe suburb. I figured I would ride out the storm with Maadi yuppies in coffee shops, then work my way north when the riots settled down. This would have been a great plan if the action was confined to downtown, but I found that no matter how far south I walked, riots and confrontations with police were taking place. Vehicles were burning, road blocks were set up by demonstrators made of cement chunks and garbage bins, a freeway interchange was on fire, there was a scorched bus and hordes of excited demonstrators near Old Cairo.

Incredibly, no matter how intense things were, everybody was polite to me and offered friendly advice about how to stay safe. One even said, "Sorry, my friend, bad time to visit Cairo." One bonus of this journey was that all along the Nile you find historic treasures such as an old palace, an aqueduct from the 1500's, and a "Nilometer" from the year 871 which measures the depth of the great river.

Large police riot trucks began convoying south along the river. They were hauling-ass and driving in a panic. In one convoy of five vehicles, all five vehicles were covered with dents from being hit with sticks and rocks. The front vehicle was dragging a traffic gate, and the next two were driving on flat tires. As they drove by crowds, people took off their shoes and beat the trucks with them. Some of the police trucks stopped to regroup. People yelled at them and tried to convince them to switch sides. I could see the panicked faces of these kids who were about 18 or 19 years old and faced with their whole society turning on them. I felt sorry for them as they argued among themselves about where to go, jumped back in their vehicles, and retreated.

A friend of mine from the hostel was trapped that same night in a small vegetable shop near Tahrir Square. He said the shop owners befriended him and gave him tea and smokes as they waited for the violence to subside. Right outside the shop window he saw about 30 police get overrun by the demonstrators. They basically had to just surrender, give up their weapons, and join the crowd to survive.

After a 10km walk, I made it to Maadi which was relatively calm, but all of the shops and hotels were closed up. I did find one vegetable stand where I bought four apples, three bottles of water, and two chocolate bars. I devoured these supplies in about 30 seconds, and then gave the apple cores to a pride of scrawny stray cats. It was an eerie vibe in Maadi and crowds began to gather. (The next night, Maadi would be the scene of looting and vigilante defense). I decided to attempt taking the subway back to my neighborhood. Miraculously, it was still working. As the subway rolled north into Central Cairo, wounded demonstrators started to board the train. One teen who had a bleeding forehead boarded the subway, stared around confused, then got off the train. Two guys carried a man onto the train who was unconscious. Another guy limped on with a broken ankle.

The train didn't stop at either of the two stations I would have normally used, Sadat Station and Nasser Station. These stations had been sealed off, and as the train sped through them the tear gas from the streets above was so bad that people had to shut the train windows. I got off the train at Orabi Station. People were hanging around the stairs looking exasperated and unsure of whether to go outside or not. Tear gas was creeping in from the street. I plotted a route back to my hostel, pulled my shirt over my nose and moved out.

The trip from the subway to the hostel was a borderline post-apocalypse nightmare scene. The dark streets were full of burned out police trucks whose wheels and engine parts had been stripped. A destroyed tow truck was still attached to a police truck which it was attempting to rescue. Broken glass and concrete rubble littered the streets in all directions. The remaining demonstrators were hard core types carrying improvised weapons, wearing surgery masks, bandanas, hoods, and saying nothing. They all drifted slowly in the same direction through a haze of smoke from various fires. In spite of some of them being wounded, they all had the confident look of a recent armed victory. Many carried captured police batons and shields and the police were nowhere to be seen. Between Orabi Station and my hostel (close to Talat Harb Square) I saw no police, even though I was well within the area which the police had meant to seal off and secure.

Many theories have already sprung up about why the police withdrew from Cairo on the night of Friday, January 28th. Some say it was an intentional move by Mubarak to foment chaos, thus making the people long for his steady hand. Some say the police were sold out by a high ranking official. But based on what I saw that night, I think the simple fact is that the riot police got their ass kicked by the demonstrators and had to get the hell out of Cairo before being totally annihilated.

The demonstrators could have easily dispersed in the face of the strong police resistance early in the day. This would have made it easy for police to successfully disburse small gatherings as they occurred, and perhaps they could have prevented any large, meaningful gatherings altogether. Instead, the demonstrators fought, some died, and they earned the right to continue to demonstrate.

Back at the hostel, the other foreigners were all glued to the TV. By then it was obvious to everyone that if you hadn't been to the pyramids yet, it probably wasn't going to happen. The next 24 hours was a band-together-in-the-fortress type scenario, as we heard gunshots, windows smashing, and occasionally a vehicle's gas tank exploding. We watched the news, tried to find ways to contact our families, and played Scrabble. (Double points were awarded for any word related to revolution).

We were running low on food and water, so the next day we got the five biggest guys together, collected money, and went foraging for food and water. A charismatic Australian bloke said he needed to show me something before we went out for food. "Mate", he said, "you've been here longer than I have, and you know these people better. You think I should bring this?" He pulled out a giant outback knife. I advised against it and pointed out that most of the people on the street only had sticks and we were twice the size of them. He agreed and we headed for the market.

All of the markets we knew of were boarded up. The "Drinkies" liquor store was being raided. In most countries' riots, the liquor store is the first shop to get hit because everyone wants free booze. In Cairo, it was being raided by guys who wanted to have a sort of "The Smashing of the Alcohol" ceremony. One renegade tried to steal a case of wine for personal consumption. They dragged him down with a crowbar, took the bottles out, displayed them to the crowd and then smashed them into the gutter. Meanwhile, the Kentucky Fried Chicken, The Adidas Store, and various other western brand name shops had been raided and many of the goods were dumped in the street. These products combined with the river of smashed booze to create a sort of infidel smoothie.

We asked around and some guys directed us to a small market which was still open. There was a bit of a "buy everything you can get before supplies run out" panic going on, but the shopkeepers were calm, polite, and didn't overcharge us by a cent. Curfew and sundown were rapidly approaching so we rushed back to the hostel. The front door of our building was guarded by a judge who was carrying a gun. Meanwhile, we noticed that every shop and building had an armed man in front of it.

The Army had entered the city, and due to the respect they have among the people, the demonstrators embraced them. As of this writing, there still hasn't been any significant Army vs. demonstrator violence, and hopefully that will continue. Unfortunately, the Army lacked the resources to protect every block and shop. So with the police gone, Cairo was ripe for looting. The men in front of the buildings were defending their homes and shops.

That night, we heard sporadic violence between looters and homesteaders. Just outside our window we heard glass smashing as a looter broke into a shop. Within minutes, he was surrounded by 10 guys carrying sticks, knives, and even numb chucks. They ranged in age from 12 to 60. They questioned the looter, and then began to beat him. Soon a man showed up with a pit bull and set him upon the looter. The looter screamed in agony, and then the men stopped beating him and pulled the dog off. After that they tied his hands and dragged him off, presumably to turn him over to the Army.

That night consisted of more gunshots, more Scrabble, and lots of tea. We made a plan to defend the hostel in case any looters came in. A French guy pulled out a small pocket knife and said, "This is a French knife." The Australian then did his best Crocodile Dundee, pulled out his outback knife and said, "That's not a knife. This is a knife."

The next morning we heard that most foreigners were evacuating Egypt. Internet was still down across Egypt, but we heard about a guy who had a satellite link. A group of us went to the place, and internet was working. We all sent hello's to our families and tried to book tickets out of Cairo. The flights to my home, Los Angeles, were all either cancelled, sold out, or ridiculously expensive. There was one exception: Aeroflot Russian Airlines connecting through Moscow. It seems I was benefitting from the fact that there had recently been a terrorist bombing in Moscow and no one else wanted to connect through there. I booked the ticket, packed my bags, showered, donned cologne and sunglasses, and proceeded to complete one last important task: I had to bring flowers to the Danish-Jordanian girl from the night at the opera. I caught a cab, and after about an hour of Army check points and skirting around debris and demonstrations, I found an open flower shop. (In Egypt, the markets, restaurants, and coffee shops might close, but the florist lives on!) I met up with her, gave her a card and the flowers and we said goodbye with plans to meet for an opera in Copenhagen, Denmark.

The cab ride to the airport was an impressive display of Egyptian military might: modern tanks at every major intersection, disciplined soldiers, and jet fighters screaming overhead.

Predictably, the airport was a scene of chaotic exodus. The Kuwait counter had a few men and large groups of wives and daughters clad in elaborate burqas. The Jordanian counter was a near violent screaming/pushing match between the 6 staff who had to link arms and the 200 customers. The whole airport was overcrowded, people in wheelchairs were getting shoved, and hustlers were scamming people out of money to "speed up" their check in. Amid the chaos there was a long, orderly line of quiet, stone-faced men wearing red jackets that said "Russia" on them mixed in with a string of gorgeous brunette and blond girls wearing ski pants. I assumed that was the line for Aeroflot and checked in. I started chatting up one of the Russkie-Lassies who was a stunning piece of work clad in a white mink coat. She had actually been to the U.S. for a year where she worked as a cashier at a roller coaster, then upgraded to waitress, and finally was promoted to being a stripper in Jersey. Given Cairo's chaos, I asked her if she was glad to be getting back to her home in Russia. She replied, "I'd rather stay in Egypt, Russia sucks."

Before boarding the plane, cell phones had been turned back on in Egypt and I was able to get a last call in to three of my Egyptian friends. One was enthusiastic about the demonstrations and wanted Mubarak to step down immediately, and for El Barradi to become President. The second wanted Mubarak to step down but was mad at the demonstrators for setting cars on fire even though the majority of the demonstrators were peaceful and well meaning. The third friend said that Mubarak had made mistakes and should be held accountable, but that he was the best option they had right now to maintain stability, and that El Barradi had been gone from Egypt for so long he had no right to be involved. Although they had different opinions, they all shared an intense love for Egypt, and saw these events as the defining moment of their generation.

3 IRAQ: A HOT DATE IN KIRKUK

On a scale of 1 to 10 I'd say Tracy was a 7 in Georgia, and a 5.5 in L.A. But I knew that a few weeks after we hit the ground in Iraq she would seem like a smoking hot 10 by comparison. Her average looks were complimented by a feisty personality, a voracious sexual appetite, and a passion for explosive demolitions. She was an Army Engineer by trade, tasked with destroying unexploded bombs and mines.

We met at Fort Benning, Georgia, known in Army cadences as "The Land That God Forgot." We were housed in a World War II era barracks where soldiers were processed en-route to war. We were all "individual augmentees" which means soldiers who basically go to war alone instead of with their normal Brigades. Individual augmentees tend to be either gung-ho volunteers, or rejects that Brigades are trying to get rid of, or just people latching on to an opportunity to radically change their destiny. Tracy, me and about 100 other desperadoes were there to postpone bad relationships, escape boring jobs, delay drunk-driving charges, and to fight for our country.

It was early 2003, and Congress was debating the decision to invade Iraq. Out of 100 soldiers, 90 of us would probably go to Iraq, 9 of us to Afghanistan, and one to Kosovo. (Lucky bastard!) On our last day before flying out, soldiers blew their money on steak dinners, booze, and strip bars. Tracy and I spent the day playing cards and making out.

None of us had been told where we going yet. Even if we were slated for the Iraq campaign, there was a big difference between a combat Battalion at the tip of the spear, and a logistics post in the rear, or even a garrison assignment in Kuwait or Qatar. In fact, at that point none of us even knew if the invasion was going to happen or not.

Eventually, me and about 8 other soldiers were gathered in a room and told we were all being assigned to a Special Forces Group. Tracy was one of the other soldiers. I had met most of the other guys that week and with one exception we all had some sort of prior operational experience. Tracy had been to Kosovo, I had been to Afghanistan, some of the others had been to the first Gulf War, and one old-timer had even been to Viet Nam. The exception was a nerdy looking Corporal whose closest encounter with combat was a backpacking trip through Europe. The poor guy had been forced to listen to a week of our war stories while suffering the unspoken recognition that he was a cherry.

A Major briefed us on the strategic situation and what to expect. Meanwhile, Tracy glanced at me, winked, and blew a kiss. I wondered if our tents would be close to one another, and I missed most of what the Major was saying. As he concluded, he asked, "Any questions?"

Tracy asked, "Just a minor point, Sir, but where are we going?"

The Major looked uncomfortable, dodged eye contact, shifted his feet, and said, "Well, I'm not supposed to tell you until you're on the plane, but …" Everyone's eyes were wide with anticipation and we all had visions of an airborne jump into Baghdad, or doing battle with the Taliban in the Afghan Mountains. "Well, ok…," mumbled the Major, "You guys are all going to Romania." There was an uncomfortable silence.

Then the Viet Nam Vet said, "Are you fucking kidding me? Romania?" It was like telling a seasoned cop that he was being assigned to rescue cats from trees.

The young Corporal proudly nodded his head and said, "Hey, I stayed at a Youth Hostel there once."

One of the desert-worthy vets of the 1st Gulf War asked, "So… if we're going to Europe, we should leave behind our desert camouflage uniforms, right?"

"Well…" said the Major, "Why don't you bring them, just in case? Yeah, definitely bring them."

Then came a barrage of questions from the group which the Major clearly didn't want to answer: "But what's the mission?"

"Which group are we being assigned to?"

"Are we invading Iraq?"

The Major, being a savvy Special Forces Officer, knew how to silence these questions by giving us unrelated information that was actually more interesting. "Let me put it to you this way; back during the Cold War, the lead commissars of the Communist Party in Russia and Eastern Europe would meet during summer at a series of luxury hotels by the beach on the coast of The Black Sea. They would partake of the finest vodka, caviar, and prostitutes available in the Soviet Empire. Then they would do a little bit of business, and go home. At present, these facilities are unoccupied and won't reopen until summer. The U.S. Government has rented them. Until further notice, your mission is to secure these luxury hotels. O.K. that's about all the time we have for questions..."

Soon, we were all on a 747 bound for Europe. There was me, Tracy, 4 other girls, and about 400 Special Forces soldiers. The competition was going to be tough. My Afghan days had taught me that unless I wanted to spend the tour watching the movie "Bring It On" I needed to dig my claws into Tracy and never let go. Within a few weeks, Tracy was getting attention from a variety of Green Berets, Navy Seals, and even British Commandos. Most of these guys were in better shape than me, had more intense jobs, and cooler looking uniforms. Typically on a military base overseas, the girls tend to favor the guys who have either the bad-ass jobs or access to alcohol. I had neither, and I was getting jealous. Fortunately, by the time the other idiots woke up to the fact that Tracy was going to be one of the base hotties, she and I had connected on a deeper level. To my pleasant surprise, she was actually very intelligent. We had many intriguing conversations, and shared a passion for getting the most out of wherever this adventure was taking us. Granted, I had some unfair advantages. For example, I ended up getting lodged in a hotel room that was only five doors away from Tracy's room. Furthermore, for the first few weeks I had no real job, so while the Special Forces guys were preparing for some secret mission, Tracy and I were on the balcony of the hotel dining on Romanian pepper steak brought up by room service, and listening to the waves of The Black Sea crash into the coast. We ended up basically moving in together and found about 64 delicious ways to kill a month waiting for whatever we were waiting for.

Sure, I did a little bit of work. I had to drive up to the capital, Bucharest, to do some business with the U.S. Embassy. The task was made more civilized by the fact that I brought Tracy as my assistant. We stayed at a 5-star hotel downtown and after experiencing a gourmet Romanian Restaurant, complete with traditional Romanian dancing, we visited ex-dictator Ceausescu's old mega-palace, and then returned to the hotel to drink a bottle of wine in the bathtub and to frolic on the biggest, most comfortable bed either of us would see for about 6 months.

The next day, I got a call from my new boss ordering me to get my "ass back to the base." Either I was in deep shit for taking Tracy on a romantic getaway, or we were about to invade Iraq. (Yes to both). Pity, we had opera tickets for that night which would have to be cancelled.

The invasion was launched from a variety of bases in countries surrounding Iraq. The group I was with launched from a Romanian Air Force Base. This base was covered with stray dogs and stray jet fighters. The jets were old MiGs; Cold War leftovers which hadn't seen a drop of lubricant since the 80's. Once the invasion decision was confirmed I finally had some real work to do planning air manifests and miscellaneous administration. It was 24/7 for a while.

Orders and messages started coming with the label "OPERATION IRAQI FREEDOM." I always objected to this label based on artistic grounds. While I understood the need to be politically correct, we were going to war and I felt a harder core operation name would be more appropriate. For example, "OPERATION DESERT SHIELD" and "OPERATION DESERT STORM" were the fantastic names for the 1st Gulf War. Better yet, the invasion of Grenada was called "OPERATION URGENT FURY." Now that's a damn good name for a mission. I suppose I should just consider myself lucky that we weren't screwed like the guys who invaded Panama with "OPERATION JUST CAUSE." That sounds like the name of a bake sale put on by Mothers Against Drunk Driving. Personally, I wanted the invasion to be called "OPERATION GREAT SATAN KICKS ASS," just to fuck with Iran. But nobody would listen to me!

I was scheduled to go down-range before Tracy, and she helped me pack my ruck-sack. She was a heck of a good packer, not a cubic inch was wasted. We knew we would see each other soon since I had booked her for an airlift soon after mine. We kissed goodbye and she jokingly said, "See you in Iraq, Dear."

I spent the next few moons leading small convoys of Toyota SUV's around Northern Iraq. I used to want to be a trucker so this was a dream job for me. We would move key personnel between fortified camps with nothing but a map, a few SUV's, grenades, and a lot of machine guns. It was basically road tripping except extremely dangerous.

But when I saw an amazing sight like the Tigris River flowing through the biblical city of Mosul, I wished I could show it to Tracy. When I smelled the oil fires of Kirkuk mixed with the scents of fly-ridden butcher shops and burning trash, I wanted to complain about it to Tracy. As I journeyed through the peaceful valleys of Kurdistan, I imagined what it would be like to take Tracy here for a weekend retreat. And when I drove through the throngs of colorfully dressed Kurdish families who gathered every Friday all along the highway to picnic and dance in the hills and rivers, I realized that this was the closest thing I'd ever seen to the parking lot outside of a Grateful Dead concert. And this made me think of … well … not Tracy. Actually, it made me think about my crazy, slutty, drug fiend, high school girlfriend Wanda. Oh, … the good old days.

In between convoys, I was tasked with miscellaneous bitch-work at our fortified camp. Although the job satisfaction was low, by now Tracy was in Iraq, and this gave me the opportunity to see her. Our romance was certainly not as cosmopolitan as it had been in Romania. The mist of The Black Sea was replaced by the dust of Iraq, and my deluxe hotel room was traded for a tent shared with 12 other guys. But Mesopotamia has a profound effect on people, and Tracy and I grew much closer in the spiritual aura of the mountains, deserts, villages, and war machines of Iraq. Nature led us to find the one hideaway on the small base that was free of other people: the pallet yard. If this were a movie, it would be a moonlit desert night blessed by a cool breeze. I would be dressed as Lawrence of Arabia, and Tracy would be dressed as an upscale belly dancer. But this is a true story, and the truth is that sex in a pallet yard sucks. On one side we had some guy stacking pallets with a forklift; on the other we had Kurdish guards bearing machine guns patrolling the base. And in our hidden spot was just miscellaneous equipment and sand. Room service was tragically unavailable.

Soon, I was sent south to Kirkuk to work on air manifests for soldiers going home. Tracy had to stay at our first base to work with some ex-Generals from the now destroyed Iraqi Army on locating minefields. We missed each other terribly.

Eventually, all of the soldiers I was meant to see on to a plane home had departed, and it was time for me to go back to the U.S. I sent word of this to Tracy. She understood, but wanted to see me one more time. Her team had a meeting scheduled with some Engineers working in Kirkuk. This gave her a chance to come to my base. We had been on hot dates together in Georgia, Bucharest, The Black Sea Coast, and Northern Iraq. Now we had the chance for one more encounter, this time in the embattled city of Kirkuk.

The day that Tracy arrived, I woke up to the sound of tanks rumbling past the air hangar which I was sleeping in. My "room" was shared with about 100 soldiers from an airborne brigade. I rolled off my cot, grabbed my M4 Assault Rifle, disassembled it, cleaned it, put it back together, dry shaved, donned my uniform and boots, made sure my dog tags were tucked into my shirt, and then went outside to piss in the weeds behind the hangar.

As I watered the weeds, I gazed out on the smoke-filled city of Kirkuk; home to Kurds, Turkmens, Sunni Arabs, Shiite Arabs, and lots of oil. Somewhere in that recipe for disaster was the U.N. compound which had a functioning non-alcoholic bar. That was the goal of our date. Tracy's boss had arranged the Engineer meeting to take place there. It was a coordination meeting, and I was basically tagging along as an additional bit of security.

I met up with Tracy and the Engineering team's "convoy" which consisted of two SUV's, and four soldiers with hand guns, including Tracy. Tracy looked damn sexy and I told her so. This was going to be a good date. The only things we were missing were some nice music, candles, and heavy weapons. My M4 assault rifle and a couple grenades were decent enough for one person but for the other 4 to only have hand guns was unnerving. I brought this up, but Tracy's boss outranked me and said "Don't worry about it." I think he had the hots' for her anyway, the dirty old perve'. We fueled up, put on flack vests and helmets, locked and loaded our weapons and rolled off the base into Kirkuk.

Kirkuk has the standard urban plan of many small Arabic cities: A central Soukh (marketplace), a huge mosque, some grand government buildings, a historic river, a "quarter" for each ethno-religious sect, and a rat's nest of intertwining alleyways and oddly angled streets which pay no heed to the cardinal directions. In other words, it's very easy to get lost. We managed to navigate our way into the central quarter which contained the U.N. Compound, but a series of road blocks forced us to take a convoluted Italian-cab style detour. We still knew where we were, but the streets seemed unusually quiet and empty.

Then the shit hit the fan. We rounded a corner and were confronted with the site of about 200 Arabs rioting and running towards us. Many of them had machine guns. The soldier driving calmly said, "That's not good." It was too late to turn around. They would have overtaken us. I aimed my M4 out the window but not directly at anyone. I tried to demonstrate that we were willing to shoot anybody who shot at us, but that we would prefer to take a pass. Tracy had her hand gun drawn. The fact was that if we started a shooting match we could have taken out quite a few of them, but we were pathetically under-gunned and they would have eventually annihilated us. Our only hope was to look ready to shoot and to drive straight through them at full speed, which is exactly what we did. They started jumping out of the way, and we managed to bull through to the far side of the riot.

We sped around another corner and had just enough time for one sigh of relief before running dead into a second riot. This group was larger, and seemed to be Kurdish. As we drove into them they were smiling, cheering, and applauding us for crashing through the Arab group. They were also heavily armed and seemed to be bent on attacking the Arabs. They waved for us to join them, an invitation which we politely declined.

We sped around another corner, breathed another sigh of relief, and promptly found ourselves heading through a third group of rioters who were being suppressed by a battle line of American Airborne Infantry and armored Humm-V jeeps with heavy machine guns mounted. This was possibly the most dangerous part of the day, since the gunner of the Humm-V would have been well within his rights to shoot us to pieces given that we were in unmarked SUV's and speeding directly at him. As soon as we saw them we slowed down and started waving the U.S. flag patches on our arms. It was a close call, but the gunner didn't shoot and as we drove by him I could see him shaking his head and mouthing "Jesus fucking Christ!!!" At the riot control line the troops were handcuffing some people and slamming a few to the ground. Beyond them there was perfect order. The airborne guys had done a great job quelling what later revealed itself to be a minor civil war in Kirkuk between Sunni Arabs and Kurds. 24 people died in the fighting on that day alone.

After all of the emergency rounding of corners, we were disoriented. It took us a few minutes to figure out where the river was, then a key bridge, and from there we could navigate to the U.N. Compound which at that point was the closest safe place we could find.

The Engineer meeting happened as scheduled. After the meeting we retreated to the non-alcoholic bar upstairs. It was a softly lit lounge with groups of well-dressed Iraqi and American politicos chatting and sipping Frescas. Some cocktail lounge music was playing and a classically attired barman said, "May I get you a drink, sir?"

"A coke for the lady, and I'll have a tonic on the rocks, please."

"Yes, sir"

It was all so civilized if you could ignore Tracy, me, and the engineers in dirty, sweaty, combat gear. Tracy and I toasted to fond memories and to not being killed in the riot. We enjoyed an extraordinarily sophisticated and peaceful 30 minutes with our drinks.

Soon, the Engineer team reconvened and someone from the U.N. introduced us to an Iraqi man who was supposed to lead us to a second meeting with another group of Engineers. He and the Engineers seemed excited to get cracking and make the second meeting happen. I hated to be a buzz-killer, but I brought up the fact that there was major rioting going on outside. Tracy's boss laughed and yelled, "Aw, fuck em', they can attack me if they want, I'm bored to death around here!" I actually admired his spirit.

The Iraqi guide shared his enthusiasm: "Don't worry," he said, "I am experienced, I have been kidnapped 7 times!"

"Well let's not go for 8 today, ok?" I replied.

Tracy's boss said, "Oh Yeah! Let's do this!" and we all went back to the SUV's. At the steps outside the U.N., 20 or so Iraqi U.N. employees were smoking cigarettes and smiling. Then we heard the crack of gunfire. They all stopped smiling and yelled, "Fire! Fire!" Then they started running in different directions, bumping into each other.

Tracy's boss was headed for a different meeting, so now it was just our one Toyota, with the addition of the Iraqi guide. After a few lefts and rights on no-name side streets we ran into, surprise, surprise, another group of rioters. This time there were only about a dozen of them, but they almost all had AK-47's. Due to the narrowness of the streets, we were driving too slowly to resort to the old crash-through technique. For a brief second, I made eye contact with one of them. We both smiled and it was sort of a "Let's just pretend we didn't see each other" agreement. We passed peacefully.

With Tracy's boss out of the picture, I was now the ranking Officer. I said Engineer meeting number two was cancelled. We drove the guide to his house, and then took the fastest route home.

Back at the base, we parked the SUV, unloaded our weapons, and took off our flack vests, helmets, and the top coat of our fatigues so we were down to boots, pants, and T-shirts. We had sweat right through our clothes, and were relieved, exhausted, and glad to be alive. After recovering for a few minutes, we got giddy and laughed and talked about the events of the day. "Can you believe that moron let himself get kidnapped 7 times?!" screamed Tracy.

"Ha-ha, but he's not as much of a moron as your boss!" I yelled.

"Fair enough," she said, "nice cocktail lounge, though, right? Whew!" Tracy's nipples were poking through her wet shirt, and one black bra strap was showing on her smooth shoulder. We walked behind a building and started making out like crazy. It had been one hell of a hot date.

4 NIGERIA: THE NIGERIAN TOP 3 LIST

Ladies and Gentlemen, the results are in:

Top 3 Names in Nigeria:

#3: Mr. Lucky! (Mr. Lucky is a pharmacist in Lagos).

#2: Mr. Bright! (Mr. Bright is a travelling salesman).

#1: Mr. Goodluck Jonathan! (Goodluck Jonathan is the President of Nigeria).

Such charming names are common in Nigeria.

Top 3 Gas Stations in Nigeria:

#3: On the road to Kaduna, in Northern Nigeria, the highway is dotted with small wooden shacks. In front of the shacks are long rows of 5-gallon fuel cans. When you need gas, you simply pull up and pay for however many cans of gas you want, and they poor them in. No pumps, no lines.

#2: At a normal gas station in Nigeria's capital, Abuja, there was a man acting like an idiot and bothering the customers. Two Army security guards approached him, and asked him to stop. He refused, and just talked a lot of trash to the guards. Then one of the guards, with expert skill, used a rope that had two steel balls on the end, to lasso the guy's feet. He pulled his feet out from under him, the guy landed on his back, and then the guard started whipping him with the steel balls. After the beating, the man jumped right back up and started yapping again. But he also decided it was time to walk away and order was restored.

#1: Coming in at #1, is the delta region of the Niger River. This region produces 2.45 million barrels of oil per day, making Nigeria the 10th largest gas station in the world.

Top 3 Expressions Heard in Nigeria:

#3: "Food-is-Ready!" If you see this sign at a road side café it means they have a batch of hot food ready to be served; and it's tasty and cheap!

#2: "The Area Boys are miscreants who may try to engage you in fisticuffs." This means that local teenage tough guys who have nothing better to do might fight you.

#1: "I will easy myself before we start driving in case there is a go-slow." This means I will go to the bathroom before we start driving in case there is a traffic jam.

Top 3 Outfits in Nigeria:

When Nigerians wear Western-style clothes, they tend to wear very conservative, dark suits. Ties and jackets are the norm in an office, even on a hot, equatorial summer day when the air conditioning is broken. When they wear traditional African dress, there is a fascinating variety of multi-colored gowns and hats, which vary based on a person's region and tribe. In the Muslim heavy north, traditional Islamic Fez hats are worn by the men and burqas and hijabs are standard for almost all women.

#3: I met a guy in my hotel named Dr. Obafemi. Dr. Obafemi was about 6' 6", massively fat, and constantly smiling. He wore a full length gown covered in big, red and green polka dots, a matching cylindrical hat, and sandals.

#2: The #2 outfit is the uniform of a typical Okoda driver. Okodas are old motorcycles which serve as a taxi. For about 50 Nigerian Naira (roughly 33 cents), they will double you on their bike just like a cab, and they are virtually everywhere. All Okoda drivers seem to wear crappy, old jeans, flip flops, and an undersized football shirt from their favorite European football team. (Usually Manchester United, Barcelona or, above all, Chelsea).

Okodas are dangerous but very handy. Sometimes, the go-slows in Lagos are so bad, that you will see a businessman get out of the back of his tinted-window SUV, and jump on the back of an Okoda to make a meeting on time.

#1: Super Mom. Many working mothers I saw used one hand to hold the hand of child, and their other hand to carry a large, heavy sack of rice. They wore large, loosely fitting gowns with bright, creative patterns. They also wore a long colored shawl which they wrapped around themselves in such a way that it created a baby backpack, and strapped an infant to their backs comfortably. On top of their heads was another shawl wrapped in such a way that it created a platform in which they balanced an even larger sack of rice. So not only was this outfit traditional, it allowed them to transport a child, a baby, and two sacks of rice.

Top 3 Ways to Die in Nigeria:

Nigeria is The World's 4th deadliest country. Here are the top 3 killers:
#3: Political Violence. Politically motivated bombings, kidnappings, and shootings are common.

#2: Disease. Nigeria is crawling with Malaria and HIV.

#1: Traffic Accidents. But while ideological killings and deadly diseases may grab the headlines, the most likely way to suffer an early death in Nigeria is actually for your poorly maintained bus to roll over, your crazy cab driver to drive onto the wrong side of the road, or for your Okoda to wipe out after hitting one of the ubiquitous, large potholes on Nigeria's highways. Highway accidents are so common that before a bus begins its journey, religious men sometimes board the bus, and offer a blessing for the journey in return for a tip.

Top 3 Most Popular Musicians in Nigeria:

Based on an informal poll which I conducted:
#3: Elton John. (I have no idea why).

#2: Fela. This classic afro-beat artist was hugely popular in the 60's and 70's, and he defines the Nigerian sound. However, I asked a younger guy if he liked Fela, and he laughed hysterically saying "Fela?! Are you kidding me? That's for old people." So if you want to be cool, you should go straight for the young people's choice and #1 on this list...

#1: MI. MI is a Nigerian rapper who you hear everywhere in Nigeria. Musically, MI isn't particularly original and he tends to just use popular hip hop sounds from the UK and USA. However, his lyrics are very powerful, and he is clearly a Nigerian singing for Nigerians. For example, in a romantic ballad about love being more important than money, he sings, "No, I don't want Naira…," and he is described as "Naija's hip hop messiah."

Top 3 Nigerian Foods:

#3: Jollof Rice. This is a delicious, fluffy rice with a meaty or vegetable sauce on top. It comes in hundreds of varieties, and is available everywhere. The meat in Nigeria tends to be cheap and tough. So I would order Jollof to fill up, get some meaty flavor, and not actually have to chew through a Nigerian meat dish. I ordered Jollof so often at my hotel that the kitchen staff asked me if I was a vegetarian.

#2: Snails. Eating snails is common in Nigeria and they don't try to hide the fact that they are garden slugs by giving them a French name.

#1: "Point-and-kill!" cafes. Outdoor garden restaurants and bars are common. You sit on plastic chairs at a plastic table set up on the grass; and enjoy the warm African air, and the sound of creatures chirping in the bush. When it's time to eat, you use the "point-and-kill!" system. That is, you chose from a selection of live chickens, fish, lobsters, or for a large family party even goats, and you point to the one you want to eat. Then they kill it, clean it, and grill it, so you are guaranteed a healthy, fresh, succulent meat dish.

Top 3 Nigerian Cities:

#3: Abuja. This is Nigeria's capital. Modern government buildings are set against stunning African rock plateaus which are covered in bright, green foliage. It is relatively safe and sanitized but it lacks Nigerian charm. The okoda motorbike taxis are banned from Abuja, but on the plus side Abuja boasts the best point-and-kill cafes.

#2: Kaduna. Mosques and churches sprinkle this relatively poor city in Northern Nigeria. But Kaduna is tourist-free, and a great way to see a real African city.

#1: Lagos. With perhaps 19 million Nigerians packed into a relatively small space, Lagos can only be described as intense. Lagos mixes oil billionaires with fishermen who live on wood platforms built up in the lagoons of Lagos. Lagos, as a do-or-die city of financial opportunity, draws people in from every region, religion, and tribe in Nigeria.

5 U.S.A.: THE GREAT ALASKAN FISHING EXPEDITION

The summer after high school, two friends and I drove to Alaska. Like the men of the late 1897 Klondike Gold Rush, we sought adventure and a chance to win our fortunes. The gold miners dug rocks out of mountains to find gold, and we scooped the guts out of fish in a cannery to earn $6/hour, plus overtime. And while the miners used sleds pulled by husky dogs, we used an 83' Toyota, pulled by an engine that had about 108,000 miles on it.

The journey began in Los Angeles. Matt and Dave, my co-adventurers, were great teammates to have for this trip. They knew how to fix cars, they had a great sense of humor, and they came equipped with a giant safari tent, high tech fishing poles, and a shotgun. According to our guidebook, fishing in Alaskan rivers would be our primary source of food.

The car was so small that after packing in our sleeping bags, the tent, the fishing poles, the shotgun case, and 6 industrial-sized cans of baked beans, we scarcely had any room left for the humans. The guy in the passenger seat had to keep two cans of baked beans between his legs, and the guy in the back had to lie down across the seat so that we could fit equipment on the floor, and then another couple of bags on top of the guy's legs in the back.

Since this was a business trip, we decided to push straight through to Alaska without wasting time on frivolities like visiting new cities, or exploring national parks. We continuously manned three battle stations and rotated every four hours: The driver was in charge of operating the Toyota safely at a fuel efficient speed, and pulling us over for gas when we reached a ¼ tank. The navigator monitored our progress on maps, made sure we took the correct roads, changed the music in accordance with the driver's wishes, and above all, made sure the driver stayed awake. The third position was the sleeper. His job was to try not to let being buried by baggage bother him, and to rest up for when he rotated into the driver's seat.

We ate on the move, usually while in the navigator's spot. We didn't need to stop to sleep since we had a sleeper position, and other than fuel stops, we only took one 45-minute break during the whole trip. (This break was in Canada, where we sampled one Canadian beer each).

Using this highly efficient system, we made it from Los Angeles to Seattle, then through Canada's British Colombia, into The Yukon Territory of Klondike Fame, across the Rocky Mountains, through Anchorage, Alaska, and finally down the Kenai Peninsula to the parking lot of The Kenai Inlet Fishing Company. Like the Clipper ships of the 19th Century, we had broken all kinds of speed records, and the total time elapsed from Los Angeles to the fish cannery was a mere 72 hours.

We walked in the front door of the fish cannery and saw a gruff, old, Alaskan, who was short, stocky, and generally grizzled. He glanced at us and said, "Who are ya', and whadya' want?"

"We're looking for jobs. We're hard-working, honest, and practical."

The guy looked us up and down and yelled, "Hired! Meet at the loading dock at 6 a.m. tomorrow. You can pitch a tent in the back lot with the rest of the rabble. FYI, the name's Tim McGavin, don't forget it."

The back lot was a nice forest sprinkled with the tents of other workers. We pitched our massive Sahara tent in a great spot. Dave had bought this tent used for $50 from a British couple that had actually camped in it in the Sahara Desert, and later in California's Mojave Desert. It had a high ceiling, plenty of room for all 3 of us, and a secondary canopy which kept out the rain and provided a storage area for our equipment and our baked beans.

At 5:45 the next morning we stood in a gaggle with about 200 other workers, all eagerly anticipating the chance to earn big money. We got to know most of these people over time. The vast majority were seasonal laborers who worked in Alaska for 6 months of the year, then returned to their home states to collect unemployment or take ad hoc jobs there. Some were ex-convicts of crimes which would get them thrown in jail in their home states, but which weren't serious enough for the law to chase them to Alaska. Roughly 50% of the people we talked in Alaska were either drunk or high.

At 6 a.m. sharp, Tim McGavin appeared, stood on a crate, and addressed the crowd. "Listen up! Every morning at 6, there's a roll call. If we need you, we'll call your name. If we don't have work for you, you go fishing. I only have three rules: #1. If you want to drink or smoke whacky-taffy after work, that's not my business. But if we catch you doin' it on the job, you're fired. #2. If you go into the fish egg room, you're fired. #3. If you don't listen to what the foreman says, you're fired. The pay is $6 per hour for the first 8 hours. After that it's $9 per hour for overtime. We just got a truck load of Salmon in, so you guys are gonna' make some big bucks! Welcome to Alaska!"

The crowd cheered and people made comments like, "Oh, this is gonna' be awesome!"

"That Tim McGavin knows what he's doing,"

"Let's gut some fish, yeah!" The Gold Rush was on.

The foreman came out, called off names, and walked us into the fish cannery. "OK, said the foreman, you're either a stacker, or a feeder, or a scooper." The stackers pulled fish out of crates and placed them on a conveyer belt. The feeders grabbed the fish and impaled them mouth-first onto a guide rod which led into a big machine which chopped off their heads and split them open down the middle. After exiting the back of that machine, the scoopers grabbed the fish, and scooped out the guts using a device that looked like an ice cream scooper which had a jet of water squirting out of it. The foreman assigned us all positions and said, "Remember, no going in there," as he pointed to a small door at the back of the factory, "That's the fish-egg room."

I was assigned to be a feeder. I felt pretty important because while they could always assign extra stackers and scoopers, there was only one spot per machine for the feeder to impale the fish. Thus, from an industrial engineering perspective, the feeder station was the limiting factor of the speed of the assembly line, and therefore, the whole group's productivity rested on my shoulders.

I wondered why they would assign the newbie to the most important job on the line. A 23-year old guy named Ryan, who had been working at the cannery since he was 16, was talking out loud to nobody in particular saying, "Yup. I've seen it all. I've seen a forklift driver work for 24 hours straight, and then he fell asleep at the wheel and drove through the back wall, right over there. The Jap's took the damages out of his pay, too. I've seen guys show up drunk and Big Tim McGavin comes in and yells at em' so bad, one guy starts cryin'. Then he fired em'. I've seen fingers get cut off, I've seen handicapped fish come down the line, I've seen…"

"Wait, Ryan, what about the fingers?" I asked.

"Heh. Heh. Yup, that's why I don't want your job," he said, as I fed the fish into the machine that axes off the fish heads. The mystery of why the new guy works as the feeder had been solved.

Dave asked, "Ryan, what do you mean by 'Japs'?"

Ryan said, "Oh, you didn't know? The company is owned by the Japanese. Yup. You're working for Tokyo, brother. Above Big Tim McGavin it's all Japanese guys." Looking at Dave and I he said, "I noticed you guys have a nice little Toyota. Next time buy American. And guess why we aren't allowed into the fish-egg room?" The door to the fish-egg room was open and we could see about 50 old Japanese ladies delicately handling fish eggs. "Yup. Our fingers are just too fat and greasy to do the job."

That night at the campfire we heated up some baked beans, and talked with a group of guys who had driven up from Minnesota. This was their second summer here. "What's with that guy Ryan?" asked Matt.

"Oh yah'," said one of the Minnesotans, "he's a weird one, yah' know. They say he survived last winter in Alaska homeless and outdoors. Hey did you guys hear the rumors about the strike? Well, the fishermen are talking about striking. If they strike that means no fish, and no work for us."

Over the next couple weeks I did my job as feeder, and when some new guys came in I asked the foreman to switch me from feeder to scooper. Gut scooping was safer and more interesting. It was a bit of an art to scoop all of the guts out without cutting into the meat of the fish itself.

The scooping section also came with some interesting challenges. For example, although the feeder station was usually the limiting factor of the assembly line there were occasions when the scoopers would fall behind. A line of five or six scoopers along a conveyor belt would scoop, but if they were too slow, the fish would coast past them and start to pile up at the back of the line, eventually spilling over onto the floor and splashing everyone's feet with guts. Then the foreman would have to shut down the line until the scoopers caught up and we would all get an ass-chewing. One time the foreman even threatened to tell Tim McGavin if it happened again. That's when everyone woke up and started to look for ways to improve our efficiency.

Dave and I talked the issue over and realized that the root of the problem was that the fish tended to come down the line in batches due to how the stackers operated with the crates. When the first fish arrived, scooper #1 would scoop it. If he finished the first fish before the second fish, he would then scoop the second fish. If not, the second fish would cruise on the conveyor belt to scooper #2, and so on. So scoopers #4, 5, and 6 tended to be underutilized at the start of a batch of fish. Then when the bulk of the batch came through, fish would eventually cruise past scoopers #1, 2, and 3 and the #4, 5, and 6 would finally have some work. But soon after, the whole line would be overwhelmed and a back-up would occur.

So Dave and I devised a system where when the first few fish from a batch came down, we would slide them back to the #4, 5, and 6 scoopers, then immediately go to work on the next few fish. This obviously resulted in better utilization of the scoopers. We got very good at sliding the fish with just the right amount of force to travel down the conveyer belt to whichever scooper was empty handed. After getting our system up and running, we never had another back up. The foreman observed us for a while and simply said, "Damn, that's good."

The only glitch in our system was Ryan. Ryan was lazy and slow, but very experienced. His experience told him that the further down the scooping line he moved, the less work he would have to do. Our system evened out the work-load, thus eliminating his sham-artist sanctuary as scooper #6. He was disgruntled. "Why're you guys passin' all the fish around?" he asked.

"Because I don't want to get fish guts all over my feet." I replied.

"Ok Mr. Fish Quarterback," he answered, "The Japs' aren't going to pay you extra or it."

We all had to listen to a certain amount of Ryan's shit because he was a six year veteran of the fish gut industry. But a couple of weeks later, a new guy named Jake showed up, and he wouldn't listen to any of Ryan's rubbish. Jake was a salty dog who ran a fishing boat. As an actual seafaring fisherman, he commanded respect among everyone in the cannery, since we were all mere landlubbers who were confined to the safety of the cannery. The only reason Jake was in the cannery was that his ship had just sunk in the Bering Strait. Everyone was in awe as he told the story of a nerve wracking three-hour sinking. He was knee-deep in icy water when another ship luckily arrived and saved him from certain death. This story trumped all of Ryan's forklift stories and Ryan was visibly upset.

Ryan started whining about the new system of fish passing again. Jake, being someone who was actually competent, really liked the fish passing system and instantly fit right into it. After Ryan babbled antagonistically about the system for about 5 minutes, Jake, without pausing in his gut scooping work, calmly said "Ryan. Listen. The reason you don't like the fish passing, is that you are lazy, incompetent, and you suck at your job. So please shut the fuck up." All of the scoopers laughed, and Ryan looked like a shorn puppy.

After a few minutes of Ryan openly demonstrating his wounded pride, we started to feel sorry for him. Then his eyes lit up and he said, "Well, Jake. Unlike you, at least I know how to float my boat!"

Everyone laughed at this, including Jake, who said, "Yeah you've got a point there Ryan."

Then Ryan, with his morale improved started singing, "Stand up and be counted, for what you are about to receive. We are the dealers, we'll give you everything you need…"and Jake and the rest of the scoopers joined in and sang the rest of AC/DC's classic song, "For Those About to Rock."

Back at the campfire, rumors of the fisherman's strike were rampant. We noticed at morning roll calls that the number of workers they needed steadily dropped from 200 one day to 160 the next to 100 the day after. One morning the foreman called out a list of about 60 names, and we weren't on the list. After roll, the foreman said, "Sorry guys, that's all for today. Try back tomorrow at 6."

"Well", said Matt, "Let's go fishing."

We got in the car and drove to a small creek which Jake had told us was running with salmon. Matt and Dave unpacked the rods and set everything up. I didn't know how to fish, so they showed me the basics and said, "Don't worry, once you feel the fish bite, instinct will take over." We sent our lines out loaded with fresh bait, hunkered down, and waited with eager anticipation to catch a bounty of fresh salmon to be grilled over the fire. Three hours later, we were still waiting. Matt said, "Well, I think this is a dry creek, maybe we should call it a day."

About that time, two local red necks showed up on the opposite side of the creek. They looked like they knew what they were doing. "Hey guys," they said, "how're you doing? Anything biting today?"

Matt said, "Nothin', man, we've been here three hours and we haven't caught a thing."

"Bummer, here have a beer." And they tossed three beers across the creek to us. About five minutes later, one of the red necks yelled, "Here we go!" His line bent towards the creek, and he started to reel something in. Soon he pulled out a beautiful, large salmon. A few minutes later his buddy caught one. Over the next twenty minutes they caught five fantastic fish and then said, "Ok, that's enough to feed the family." Then they packed up, said, "Good luck," and moved on.

Matt and Dave were suffering from fisherman's wounded pride, and Matt said, "We're not leaving here until we catch at least one fish." About an hour later, Dave got a tug on his line. Excited, he pulled and reeled in. Could this be the catch of the day? He reeled and reeled, and out of the water came a little fishy about 4 inches long. We were massively disappointed and there was an uncomfortable silence. Then Matt yelled, "Hey, we caught one!" and we all cheered, packed up and drove back to the cannery.

That night we started a fire, cleaned and gutted Moby Dick, and roasted him over the fire. The fish provided us with about 1 mouthful each of fish. This was our "primary source of food," that the guidebook had mentioned.

The next day there was no work again. We were standing next to Michael, Louise, and Freda, a trio from Baltimore who only wore gothic, all-black clothes and white makeup. They were usually either discussing death or singing songs by The Cure. A hippie from Oregon walked by them and said to a friend, "Hey, it's gonna' be a sunny day, my guitar is alive, and we've got a million acres of Alaskan Wilderness to explore. All right!" Michael, Louise, and Freda scowled at him and shook their heads.

Michael said, "Great. There goes another I-love-lifer."

I figured these three weren't prone to excessive optimism so I asked them what they'd heard about the strike. "Not only is there a strike," said Louise, "but this has been one of the worst fishing seasons in ten years. No one wants to admit it, but the whole system is going to collapse. Even that psycho Tim McGavin is going to lose his job!"

Freda said, "Um. Yeah. I hope so."

Then Michael said, "Why are we even talking about this? Does it even matter whether the fish swim in the sea, or the birds fly in the sky, or the fishermen have the metaphysical insight to realize that they are being exploited!? Does it even matter considering we only make six fucking dollars an hour, and we'll blow that anyway on liquor and drugs before we even get back to Baltimore?"

"Oh," said Louise, "And don't forget to buy a narcissistic 'I fished in Alaska' T-shirt so that everyone in Baltimore knows how cool you are."

Then Freda started singing, "I've been looking so long, at these pictures of you, that I almost believe that they're real."

A week went by with no work and the labor camp was getting restless. At first, many people just read their books, usually John Steinbeck's Cannery Row. Then people started drinking heavily during the day and the ping pong table in the break room always had a long line.

Gordon, a 50-year old motor-biker, would hang out by the ping pong table and tell everybody either about the technical specifications of his Harley Davidson or about his ill-fated bike ride to Mexico. "The Mexican cops pulled me over, searched my bags, and found 1 marijuana joint … 1. Then they took me to jail for 2 years. 1 joint … 2 years … 1 joint … 1."

Another jobless week went by and people started complaining to Tim McGavin. Some people were blaming everything on "The Japanese," and the camp was approaching disarray. Then, at the critical point when things were about to collapse, Ryan was seen walking around the camp saying, "Hey everybody, there is a meeting by the fire pit at 2 p.m. Big Tim McGavin said so!"

At 2, all the workers gathered, and Tim McGavin stood up on his crate. "All right guys, I'm not going to lie to you. As long as the fishermen are on strike, there'll be no fish, and if there's no fish, there's no work for us. I know you're tired of this! I know you wanna' work! I know you're hungry! I know you dropped everything and crossed The Rocky Mountains because you just want to make a living! I know you're sick of this strike and God Damn it, so am I!!!"

The crowd was yelling "Yeah!"

"Say it, brother!"

"Right on, Tim McGavin!"

"And let me tell you," he continued, "Soon you're gonna' see a giant 18-wheeler truck pull into that driveway so loaded down with fresh fish that it can barely move. The icy water's gonna' be drippin' off those crates, the forklift is gonna' stack em' up in front of the line, you're all gonna' gut those babies out, and then you're gonna' get paid a lot of money!!!" The crowd cheered wildly. Then Tim McGavin toned it down a bit, calmed the crowd, and said, "But until then we gotta' stay cool. Oh, and I ordered up a little Alaskan style lunch for ya', enjoy." And then the foreman and a few other guys started bringing out trays and trays of fresh, grilled salmon. Tim McGavin pulled up his pick-up truck, opened the doors and started blaring country music. The workers dug into the fish vigorously, and there was so much of the delicious, pink, Alaskan salmon that we couldn't even finish it. After the feast, people sat around saying, "That was the best salmon I've ever eaten."

"Tim McGavin is awesome."

"I can hold out here for a long time, the fish will come in any day now."

All of this bought Tim McGavin about one week. But the strike continued, and the workers still had no income. Drunkenness returned to the camp. More and more people started to associate with the pessimists Michael, Louise, and Freda. People started breaking into other people's tents and stealing things. Some fist fights broke out.

Matt, Dave, and I had a strategic conference. We did the math, and realized that another week of lost wages plus the imminent threat of camp violence wasn't balanced by a good salmon feast. Not to mention, we were sick of baked beans, and couldn't catch Alaskan fish to save our lives. We unanimously agreed to the following course of action: "Let's get the fuck out of this place."

We packed up and gave our leftover beans to Ryan who was overwhelmed by the gesture and just said, "Yup. Guys…ride on."

We drove up the Kenai Peninsula again, through Anchorage, over the Rocky Mountains, and into the Yukon Territory. I made some phone calls en-route and lined up a construction job at my uncle's farm in Canada. The pay was better than in Alaska, and my Aunt fed me delicious gourmet dishes every night.

Matt and Dave made their way back to California to start a used car business which quickly failed, and then they got busted for fishing without a license by California park rangers. They spent the rest of the summer drinking and going broke.

Our Alaskan adventure was a total failure. We suffered a net loss financially, and we had wasted a lot of valuable time. But we had achieved a historical connection to the old Gold Rush men since our fate was very similar to the fate of the vast majority of miners who thronged to Alaska and The Yukon in 1897. Most of them never found anything but fool's gold, and after failing as miners they wound up penniless, lonely, and drunk.

6 LEBANON: COFFEE WITH HEZBOLLAH

Lebanon has some incredible Roman ruins. If these ruins were in Italy they would be major tourist attractions, but since everyone is afraid to travel to Lebanon, they go unnoticed. My goal for the day was to visit the Roman ruins of Baalbek.

I found a group of idle taxi drivers and started to negotiate the fare for a round-trip ride of several hours to Baalbek. All the taxis in Lebanon are Mercedes Benz's. These guys had luxurious, late model Benzo's and they were asking for more money than I was willing to pay. I bargained with them, and they brought their price down, but not by enough. So I thanked them and started to walk away. Then they said, "Wait, wait, we can meet your price, but you have to go with Riyadh." They pointed to Riyadh, a short, ugly man with a giant wart on his nose. His Mercedes looked like a 1982 model, and it was as rusty and scruffy looking as its owner. But the price was right, so I said, "Let's go to Baalbek, Riyadh." He gave a big smile and fired up the 82' Benz.

We fought our way through the heavy traffic of cosmopolitan Beirut. Beirut is a unique blend of mosques, churches, chic boutiques, stylish coffee shops, and sexy, olive-skinned divas who speak French when they feel like it. The aromas of Beirut vary from cologne and perfume, to savory Lebanese cooking, to automobile exhaust, to cigarette and shisha smoke.

The soccer World Cup was starting in a few weeks and all across Beirut were thousands of national flags representing the different countries competing. Lebanese are an international trading people, and most have one foot in some other country like Brazil, Germany, U.S.A., or Nigeria. Whether this is due to a historic connection with the ancient Phoenician sailors, or the Arabic caravan merchants, or whether it's a result of Lebanon's unique geographic position at the edge of both the Mediterranean Sea and the Middle

East, is open to debate. But it's a fact that Lebanese people are a major part of the business elite of Brazil and Africa, and they have a significant presence throughout Europe and North America. So a guy who has a cousin in France cheers for the French team in the World Cup. If he owns part of a business in Brazil he has a Brazilian flag on his Mercedes. And if he went to school in Canada he wears a Montreal Canadians hockey jersey.

As we left Beirut we said goodbye to the Mediterranean Sea and climbed up the beautiful mountains into Lebanon's interior. I wasn't sure if Riyadh's taxi could handle the trip uphill, and there was lots of chugging and shaking. He kept patting the dashboard and telling me, "She is a great car."

Riyadh started to give me his unsolicited opinion of politics. I tried to avoid the subject of politics like the plague while I was in Lebanon, but people bring it up all the time. He gave me a long story about the Israeli bombings of 2006 and how many innocent people were killed. I heard this very often, but only rarely did anyone talk about the innocent people killed by rockets fired into Israel from Southern Lebanon. I heard plenty about "Israeli Apartheid" against Palestinians, but no one ever talked about the fact that Palestinians who have lived in Lebanon since 1948 are still legally barred from holding jobs or buying property, and are basically treated as second class citizens. The rationale is that if they are treated as citizens they will never go back to Israel.

The Shia Muslims I knew said the Israeli bombings were massive and indiscriminate. The Sunni Muslims told me that originally the bombs were just aimed at Shia neighborhoods, and it wasn't a big deal. But it spread to Sunni neighborhoods and this was ridiculous. The Christians I knew said they were precision strikes against targets that had been involved with attacking Israel. They were so certain of where the strikes would be that they had rooftop parties to watch the bombings.

We crested the mountains and descended into the wide, fertile, Beqaa Valley. At a fork in the road, one sign pointed to Syria, and the other to Baalbek. Riyadh took the Baalbek road, and soon we were headed into the territory of Hezbollah. Hezbollah means "Party of God." It is an Iranian-backed organization which politically represents and provides social services for Shiite Muslims in the Beqaa Valley. It also acts a terrorist organization, and got its start in the 1980's kidnapping Americans and other Westerners. Along the road side I saw many billboards showing legions of uniformed, trim-bearded Hezbollah soldiers. Quaint agrarian villages were mixed with occasional "camps" which were clusters of shacks. Baalbek itself was a city with a mix of nice homes, some disheveled lodgings, a solid downtown core of 3-story buildings, and plenty of beautiful mosques.

At the entrance to the Roman ruins, a cluster of guys tried to sell me souvenirs including a Hezbollah T-shirt. They seemed disappointed that I didn't want to buy the T-shirt. I guess they didn't realize that in the unfortunate event that I became owner of a Hezbollah T-shirt, I would use it in the same way a Che Guevara T-shirt deserves to be used; namely, as toilet paper.

The ruins themselves were phenomenal. They were likely the central, public core of a large Roman city and included an amphitheater, several places to worship Roman Gods, a large market, and a local Senate. There was even a chamber dedicated to Bacchus where supposedly, Romans would bring their wives and engage in all manner of hedonistic debauchery.

After the grandeur of old Rome I was ready for a serious feeding session. I told Riyadh I was going to one of the restaurants next to the ruins. He said I shouldn't go there because they were way too expensive, and that they existed solely to rip off the hordes of rich tourists who come to Baalbek. I looked around and counted 7 other tourists total at the ruins.

"Come, I buy you lunch, my friend," said Riyadh. We walked a few blocks into the core of the city. I figured this would be the scene where I get kidnapped for being American or for failing to buy a Hezbollah T-shirt.

Amidst a confusing bazaar cluttered with merchants selling all manner of electronic gadgets, chickens, and carpets, Riyadh found a hole in the wall butcher shop that had a large lamb carcass hanging near the doorway. Riyadh negotiated with the owner for about 10 minutes, not about price, but about which part of the animal he wanted. They pointed at different parts of the animal and finally settled on some part of the leg. The butcher hacked off a big chunk of meat, and ran it through a hand-powered meat grinder. Meanwhile his assistant was making little circles of dough and laying them out on a tray. Then they put big morsels of the meat onto the dough circles, wrapped each one into a ball, and put the entire tray into a large, open hearth which had a fire burning.

10 minutes later we had a bag full of the most delicious meat snacks I've ever had. Can meat get any fresher than watching it go from the animal itself and turning into lunch before your very eyes? I was really impressed. Riyadh paid and the batch of snacks they made for us was more than enough to fill up Riyadh and I, and he even still had a bag of leftovers to bring to his wife.

Feeling fat n' happy we started to drive back. But on the Southern edge of Baalbek, I saw an ornate mosque which was particularly intriguing for some reason. I wanted to get a closer look without actually going onto mosque property. There was a small coffee shop next door with a tin roof, so I had Riyadh pull over. The coffee shop was ratty and dingy on the outside, and the owner eyed me suspiciously. I greeted him politely in Arabic and asked if I could drink some nice coffee. He smiled brightly and switched into Arabic hospitality mode. He showed me into the coffee shop whose interior was mysterious, dark, and cluttered with old leather couches and shisha pipes. I was the only customer. The owner brought me an ancient, finely decorated coffee pot which was filled with extremely strong Turkish coffee. I bought one for Riyadh also, and the owner sat with us and chatted. Soon three or four other hangers-on sat down with us. (Every coffee shop and cigarette shop has a few unemployed guys who lounge around and help their cousin run the place).

I asked about the mosque which had caught my eye. They were very excited to talk about it and they gave me a long story about how Ali, the fourth Caliph, had a wife who gave birth by the river next to the mosque. As a result, for over 1,000 years Shiite Muslims have made pilgrimages to this spot to partake of the holy river water and to pray at the mosque.

Then, again without my prompting, the discussion turned to politics. They spoke passionately about how great Hezbollah was, and how Baalbek had been hit particularly hard by the Israeli bombings. Many of their friends had died, but they were happy because they had fought back by firing rockets into Israel. At the mention of this, they started smiling happily and clapping.

I really wanted to change the subject so I said, "How 'bout that World Cup!?" Then they talked about how great the German and Spanish teams were. And they spoke with even more passion about the World Cup than about Hezbollah, and again smiled and clapped, yelling "Go Germany!" This reminded me of an S-class Mercedes I saw in Beirut which was covered in German flags and had a large swastika painted on the hood. It's not the fault of modern Germans, most of whom want nothing to do with Nazism, but several Lebanese I met denied the existence of the holocaust and painted Hitler in the most progressive, visionary light possible.

After 2 cups of Turkish coffee, which is enough to keep you awake for 4 days, we headed back to Beirut. I tipped Riyadh big, and told him to buy a new muffler. His Mercedes had done the job, the Roman ruins of Baalbek were still there, Hezbollah didn't kidnap me, I learned about a historic mosque, and I had tasted the most delicious meat snack ever invented. It had been a great day in beautiful Lebanon.

7 AUSTRALIA: Y2 G'DAY

December 23rd, 1999: "Holy Shit! That was a kangaroo!" I yelled.

"Are you kidding me?" replied my buddy Steve. In a panic, he nearly crashed the car as we pulled over to get a photo of the kangaroo. We still hadn't mastered driving on the left side of Australia's highways and random sightings of exotic wildlife made things worse. By the time we pulled over and got out of the car with our cameras, the kangaroo had bounced off into the outback. Disappointed, we put away our cameras, and took the opportunity to urinate. About half way through this procedure, four other kangaroos started bouncing past us. With my pants unzipped, and in midstream, I fumbled for my camera, twirled around, and snatched a perfect shot of four beautiful kangaroos jumping across the Australian desert. We were hoping to see the stereotypical mama kangaroo with a baby in her belly pouch, but it didn't happen.

We got back into the car and continued our road trip from Sydney to a magical place called "Surfer's Paradise" on Australia's Gold Coast. We were jacked up on kangaroo adrenaline and unfortunately this resulted in our driving at an excessively high rate of speed. In no time, a police car pulled us over for speeding. I thought Aussie cops would be unshaven bad-ass mo-fo's who were raised on Mad Max movies. But this chap was more in line with the Commonwealth "bobby" type of policeman. He gave us our ticket and said, "Since you blokes are foreigners we can do fuck all about it if you don't pay the bloody ticket. So my advice is don't pay it, and keep it as a souvenir of Australia. Cheers, mate!" We were so grateful for his honesty that we obeyed the speed limit for the rest of the trip.

December 26th, 1999: We stopped for gas, and bought a stuffed kangaroo who we named "Matey-the-Kangaroo." Matey became our

Aboriginal talisman and provided luck and good fortune for the rest of the trip.

Across the street we saw a rickety wooden building with a dusty old sign saying, "PUB." Other than the gas station and this building there was nothing but windy desert and a gathering of shabby homes. Apparently, this was the central business district of beautiful Nowheresville, Australia.

Naturally we investigated the pub. It was dustier inside the pub than outside, and the ambiance reminded me of old Australian Outback movies like Crocodile Dundee and the Man From Snowy River. Behind a large, oak bar, we saw the smiling face off an old, short, fat blond woman who welcomed us heartily and poured us a couple of pints.

"Where're youz' guys from?" she asked.

"America. We're driving up to Surfer's Paradise."

"Good on ya', mates," she said, "I used to go up there on me' holidays just to sit on the beach and perve' on all the lifeguards."

Out of the blue, a bass voice from a dark corner of the bar yelled, "You American blokes all think you're heroes, don't ya'!" We looked over and saw an Aussie about 6'2" staggering towards us. He looked about 25, unshaven, ill-groomed, and he smelled like he'd been wandering around the desert drinking for several days. After an uncomfortable silence, he reiterated "…..alllllll heroes, eh?" and walked within a foot of my friend Steve who was also about 6'2" and built like a tank.

"What are you talkin' about, dude?" replied Steve.

"Don't pretend you don't know what I mean, yank."

A short aborigine guy in a rugby jersey popped up and said, "Mates, you gotta' watch out for Glen, eee's a wild one."

Steve and this Glen stared each other down and it looked like a bar room brawl was imminent. Just then the woman tending the bar yelled, "God damn it, Glen! Don't come in here makin' trouble with my customers! I'm sick of your substance abuse! Go back to your trailer and sleep it off, you'll feel better!" It was a pretty good ass-chewing.

Glen looked at her and said, "You've got a point, there." Then he glared right at Steve's nose and coolly said, "Next time, duck, mate."

Steve started laughing out loud and said, "That's fantastic. He can tell my nose has been broken."

Glen started laughing as well, offered a handshake to us and said, "Glen's the name."

We had introductions all around and started drinking heavily with Glen and the Aborigine guy whose name was Jim. We talked about rugby and beer, and after a while Glen said, "Let's grab a box of beer and go drink it by my trailer. This bird charges too much!" That comment sparked another ass-chewing from the bartender and we paid our tab and said goodbye.

December 27th, 1999, City of Surfer's Paradise: The end of The World was rapidly approaching. Pundits, street corner prophets, and IT gurus all predicted mass chaos to result from the dreaded Y2K virus which would kick in at midnight, December 31st, 1999, as a result of computer clocks being programmed with 2-digit years, and thus not being able to distinguish the year 2000 from the year 1900. Planes would crash, stock prices would tumble, and orders for Big Macs would be filled by Chicken McNuggets.

In a normal year, The City of Surfer's Paradise is dedicated to drunkenness, debauchery, crazy sex, and of course, surfing. But with the approach of impending doom, the city's hedonistic style took on a Last Days of Rome character. We spent four insane nights reveling in the madness, and the Australian people more than justified their reputation for being the craziest partiers on earth.

December 31st, 1999, Sydney: Due to its time zone, Sydney is one of the first major party cities to celebrate New Year's Eve. At about 10 a.m. each year, North Americans who are still picking up their New Year's Eve outfits from the dry cleaners can get a glimpse on TV of life in the next year. But this year was different. Sydney would be a test of whether the Y2K virus was real. More importantly, Australians would be one of the first to have a great party in a new millennium … something the human race can only do every 1,000 years.

The center of the action was the Sydney Opera House, the giant Sydney Harbour Bridge, and a notorious heavy drinking district known as The Rocks. Throughout the day swarms of people from all over the world streamed towards The Opera House. Steve and I arrived early and packed ourselves right by the water with some bread, a jar of the Australian delicacy Vegemite, and 12 Victoria Bitter Australian beers. After several hours we had to take a leak. We turned around and saw what looked like tens of thousands of revelers crammed in behind us like so many drunken sardines. We were trapped. Going to the bathroom was not an issue since our spot was adjacent to the water. But on a more serious note, we had run out of beer and vegemite.

Luckily for us, I had brought Matey-the-Kangaroo, and lodged him in between my chest and my top button so that just his head and arms stuck out under my chin. Girls gravitated to Matey. One girl pointed at Matey and yelled, "Chick Magnet!" I said, "Yeah, and the Kangaroo is cute, too." This led to a conversation about the end of the universe and we found out that she and her friend were New Yorkers. True to Big Apple style, they had sharp wit, sexy outfits, perfect bodies, bitchy attitudes, bags under their eyes, and worn out skin which demonstrated a history of excessive stress and lack of sleep. In addition, they had food, wine, and a giant blanket. The five of us spent the next few hours boozing and feeding, and soon midnight was upon us.

The crowd counted down to midnight with a hysterical accent, and as Y2K, and a new set of 1,000 years arrived, gigantic fireworks exploded in the sky, The Sydney Harbour Bridge lit up, and we made out with the New York chicks like bandits.

At about 3 a.m., the girls said goodnight and things took a turn for the worse. The decent people had all gone home, and The Rocks turned into a swarm of derelicts just like us. We drifted into a pub, there was a fight somewhere, and Steve vomited all over the floor. An Aussie looked at him, shook his head, and said, "Go home ya' bloody yank." We left the pub and noticed that an Irish guy we had talked to earlier was sleeping on top of the rubbish bins. Matey-the-Kangaroo was lost, probably drowning somewhere in the river of booze, piss, and vomit, that now filled the gutters.

But all of this was a mere warm up to the real purpose of our voyage: Inter-Millennial Time Travel. We headed for the airport.

January 1st, 2000, Sydney Airport, 8 a.m.: Our QANTAS Airways flight took off, bound for Honolulu, Hawaii, apparently uninhibited by the evil Y2K virus. The majority of the passengers were passed out drunk as the plane made the ten hour journey to Hawaii. About half way through the flight we crossed The International Dateline. (Side note for the geographically disinclined: The International Dateline is 180 degrees around the globe from Greenwich, England where the time change is 0. Paris is +1, Moscow is +4, Shanghai is +8, etc. In reverse, New York is -5, Los Angeles is -8 etc. Eventually this loss of hours and gain of hours meets in the middle of the Pacific Ocean. As you cross The International Dateline from the +12 time zone to the -12 time zone, you lose a full day. This effect of losing 1 day is what allowed Phileas Fogg, the hero of Around the World in 80 Days, to win his bet for 20,000 English Pounds that he could circumnavigate the globe in 80 days or less).

Due to our crossing The International Dateline, we landed in Honolulu Airport, Hawaii at 10 p.m., on December 31st, 1999.

December 31st, 1999, Waikiki, Hawaii, 10:49 p.m.: We took a cab back to my apartment, dropped our bags off, donned Hawaiian shirts, and rushed over to my neighbors pad, unshaven and un-showered. (Time was of the essence!) She was having a raucous end of the world party. The crowd in her living room was out of control and they were all partying like it was 1999. I jumped up on a table and yelled, "I have an important announcement to make! We've just travelled here from The Year 2000 … AND WE'RE STILL ALIVE!!!!" People cheered wildly and high-fived each other.

Our party moved as a mob down to Waikiki Beach, where thousands had gathered to be one of the last cities to welcome The New Millennium. As the crowd counted down from ten, people were running into the warm sea, kissing each other, crying, and howling with joy. Fireworks hung in the air, and I spent ten minutes kissing some girl who seemed to come from out of the ocean.

As the fireworks died down, people wandered back through the streets of Waikiki yelling, "Aloha!" and hugging complete strangers. A purple glow hung over the city, and after the exuberant vibes of Sydney and Honolulu, it was clear that humanity was destined for 1,000 new years of exploration, passion, adventure, and love.

8 CHINA: THE HARD SEAT TRAIN TO KASHGAR

In China, the long distance rail options are a bit different than 1st class, Business Class, and Coach. You can choose Soft Sleeper, Soft Seat, Hard Sleeper, or Hard Seat. Hard Seat is the cheapest, and as the name implies, you get a hard seat to sit on and that's about it.

I boarded the train in Shanghai; China's cosmopolitan business epicenter, and my destination was Kashgar. Both in the colonial era, and in modern times, the tendency of western visitors has been to stick to the large, modern, coastal cities of China. So just to be different, I decided to shoot for Kashgar, which is on the extreme, western edge of China. I bought a Hard Seat ticket from Shanghai to Xian, which was about 1/3 of the way west across China. The route passed through a series of smaller Chinese cities. In China, "smaller cities" really means a massive sprawl of factories, warehouses, and apartment blocks holding about 1 to 5 million people. (China has 200 cities of 1 million or more people!)

A Chinese trader of about 50 started talking to me. He had been to Shanghai for a vacation with the woman sitting next to him. Then the woman said, "I wanted to stay in Shanghai, but his wife wants him back. I'm his lover." They were being all cuddly and kissy and it was mildly repulsive. They were also gorging on a bowl full of chicken feet. They offered me some but I explained that I was allergic to chicken feet.

A younger couple from some city halfway to Xian started talking to me. I asked them if they went to Shanghai for business, and the girl said, "No way! We went for pleasure!" and then they got cuddly and kissy.

I got some tea from the dragon lady who is in charge of the hot water, then settled in to watch the story of China unfold. At Xian, I headed straight for the Terracotta Warriors. This life size, 8,000-man underground army is absolutely surreal. Emperor Qin Shi Wang constructed these men in 210 BC in order to protect himself during the afterlife. Seeing this mysterious creation takes you back through Chinese history and this site alone makes the trip to Xian worthwhile.

I rode the bus back in to central Xian, and explored the giant city walls. These fortifications were started by The Ming Dynasty in 1370, and dwarf any similar walls which you might find in Europe. They are 4 stories high, 45 feet wide and 14 km long! Once on top, I took in a great view of the city of Xian, and climbed through one of the creepy, old guard towers. Once back on the wall, I was seized with the urge to do a complete circle around the city on top of the walls.

It was a long, cold, bitter, and windy walk. But the view from the walls kept me going, and every kilometer there was an interesting historical plaque. About 2/3 of the way around, I was pretty exhausted. I was close to a major gate and decided to take a break.

The massive gate enclosed a courtyard the size of half a football field. In this courtyard, there were about 50 Mini-Cooper sports cars with bizarre, multi-colored paint jobs. The cars were buzzing around in circles, a DJ was playing, and an MC was giving medals out to the victors of some competition.

There was a café in the corner of the courtyard, and I walked in to warm up and get a cup of Chinese tea. The barista spoke some English and explained to me that there had been a long distance motor rally with the 50 Mini-Coopers and this was the finish line and closing ceremony.

The crowd in the coffee shop was an eclectic mix of people including drivers from the rally, audio techs who had set up the closing ceremonies, a few slick promoters in sharp suits, and nine fashion models all wearing slinky, angelic, white dresses.

I enjoyed the atmosphere and my tea, and then continued with the long march. The last leg of the journey was a miserable contrast to the warmth and sex appeal of the Mini-Cooper rally. The sun had set, the wind had picked up, and I was the sole remaining tourist on top of the walls. But the physical hardship of the trek was overcome by the aura of mystery created by thousands of traditional Chinese lanterns which light the wall up at night. After dark, it is easy to forget that you are surrounded by a modern city. The 14 kilometer string of lanterns, the thick stone walls, and the eerie memories of The Terracotta Warriors, all combined to take one back through the centuries to when Xian was one of the largest and most powerful cities in the world.

I trudged on and eventually reached another gate. I wanted to go down the stairs, but the exit was closed off. Apparently, it was past business hours, and I was trapped on top of the walls. I was bitterly cold at that point, and unfortunately, the ancient emperors had done a proper job of building the walls such that it was impossible to climb up or down them. I figured I would walk to the next gate in the hopes of finding a different way to get off of this historical merry-go-round. Worst case scenario, I would have to walk around in circles until sunrise to stay warm. Then, from about 3 kilometers away, I saw a golf cart slowly cruising towards me along the top of the wall. It was security doing an end of day sweep for errant tourists. He gave me a ride to another gate, let me out, and I headed for the train station.

I bought a ticket from Xian to Urumqi, this time a Hard Sleeper. I caught some shut eye as we rolled west and woke up when the train pulled in to the city of Jiayuguan. On the train station platform there was a ten foot long miniature model of an ancient Chinese fortress which I could see without getting off the train. It was fascinating, and I wanted to see the life size version of this fortress. About ten minutes after pulling out of the station, we passed the real thing. It was a large, intimidating fortress, and its defenses pointed due west. It was constructed in 1372, during the Ming Dynasty.

At the time, the city of Jiayuguan was the western edge of the Chinese world. Beyond this were only "barbarians." The Jiayuguan fortress was the last outpost on the frontier of civilization. And to this day, although it is only about half way west across China, over 95% of China's population lives east of Jiayuguan. Eastern China's factory cities, farms, and canals, are replaced by forbidding desert and mountain landscapes. Although there are islands of large industrial cities populated mostly by Han Chinese in Western China, they are isolated in a sea of uninhabitable terrain, and by large regions populated with traditional Muslim cultures such as The Uighurs, and The Hui who earn their living either farming, raising livestock, or trading with neighboring Central Asian countries.

The journey to Urumqi was harsh and monotonous, edging along the Gobi desert, and advancing up the ancient Silk Road trading route, once travelled by Marco Polo. In elementary school, I was always confused when they taught us that Christopher Columbus risked a dangerous sea journey and falling off the edge of the earth just to find an alternate route to China. Why bother when there is an established land route? But after seeing the misery and danger of the best pre-1492 route first hand, it was easy to appreciate the desire to find an easier path.

The modern Silk Road consists of the railroad I was using, and a modern highway which carried an endless stream of large trucks. Every so often along the highway there was a gas station, usually with a mosque built next door. This was a good indication of the transition from Han China to Western China. Many of the truckers were probably Muslims from Uzbekistan and Kyrgyzstan, or the Uighur and Hui groups. Perhaps they were direct descendants of the many ancient Muslim caravans which for centuries plied the route of the Silk Road between China, Central Asia, and The Middle East.

Urumqi was a large, cold, industrial city with long, wide streets connecting apartment blocks to massive factories. I bought some souvenirs, ate a few dumplings, and tried to get a ticket to Kashgar. The train station was jam packed and each of the 20 ticket booths had a line of about 70 people. The train schedule was all in Chinese. I looked in my guidebook which had Kashgar written in English next to the equivalent Chinese characters. Then I matched these characters to the board and found a train to Kashgar. Since I had plenty of time to kill waiting in line, I also decoded the words for 1-way ticket and Hard Seat. Then I transcribed these onto a sheet of paper to hand to the ticket agent. While waiting in line, I saw some guy try to cut the line (in front of all 70 people), and a fist fight broke out as a result. Police came over and settled the issue, and nobody else tried to cut.

Eventually I got to the front of the line, and with 70 people now crowding behind me; I prayed that my first effort in writing Chinese characters would work. The ticket agent took my sheet and my money, and a few seconds later I had a ticket of some sort in my hand. I spent about 10 minutes in a corner of the station decoding the ticket, and eventually found that, indeed, I had the right ticket and was on my way to Kashgar.

The next 24 hours were a dazzling display of western Chinese dramatic scenery. Deserts, cliffs, mountains, and dusty Uighur villages all passed by. Once in Uighur and Hui territory, hours at a time could pass without seeing modern buildings, and it was easy to imagine that I was back on the old Silk Road. Then out of the blue a giant mine or factory would appear. On one twisty, mountainous section of the journey, a gargantuan half-finished bridge rose from out of nowhere in the desert, up to meet the train tracks which were halfway up the side of a mountain. The mix of ancient Muslim civilizations, desert, and the rapid expanse of heavy industry was surreal.

A Chinese student of about 21 started talking to me. He was studying engineering in Beijing, China's cultural treasure and political capital. For him, it was a great feat to be able to get a place in university and to move from his mid-sized home city somewhere in Eastern China to Beijing, the center of the action.

But now, he explained, most of his graduating class was having a hard time finding a job in The East. He had journeyed by train all the way from Beijing to go to a job interview at a factory somewhere in between Urumqi and Kashgar. He desperately wanted to stay in Beijing, or at least somewhere in the eastern half of China, but the jobs were steadily moving west.

A platoon of Chinese Army soldiers got on the train, about 40 in all. Except for a handful of officers and older sergeants, the soldiers all looked about 18 and wore clean, new, high tech uniforms. The discipline of the junior soldiers was very tight, but the officers and sergeants spent most of the trip drinking heavily and eventually passed out in comical positions with bits of their uniforms falling off.

As we journeyed west, the soldiers and engineers got off the train, and were replaced by Uighur farmers, who had a Turkic or Caucasian appearance. As the Beijing engineering student was getting off the train he said, "Be careful of these people getting on the train, they are Uighur people."

A family of 11 boarded, led by one toothless, tough looking, middle-aged man in a wool coat and cylindrical wool hat. They made a lot of commotion and changed seats five or six times before settling in with a massive amount of luggage. The father (or grandfather) had an argument with an old Chinese man who kept farting and belching, and had his smelly feet up on the seats. Then the Uighur's wife ran off a fragile Chinese woman of about 65 who looked very poor and confused. She tried to find a place to put her bag, (which carried some sort of vegetable crop), but no matter where she put it, the whole Uighur family, from grandfather to 6-year old daughter, would yell at her, and keep the space for their own luggage. The woman was at a loss, so I shoved some of the Uigher family's luggage aside and put the woman's baggage up in the rack. The Uighur leader gave me a mean look and I said, "Hello" in Uighur, (I had just looked it up in my guidebook). He laughed out loud at this and then all his offspring crowded around me and made me say more Uighur expressions. I also knew, "How are you?" but that was it.

A girl of about 12 had a Mickey Mouse jacket on. She reached into my bag and helped herself to a book about The Napoleonic Wars. Her brother, about 16, showed me his watch and gold chain, and although he didn't speak English, he somehow communicated to me that all the Uighurs on the train were headed into Kashgar for the big Sunday bazaar. They were going to sell some things, buy some things, visit cousins, and have fun in Kashgar, the epicenter of the Uighur world.

I noticed that the Mickey Mouse girl was reading my book from right to left. The Uighur language is related to Arabic, and they read right to left, so the girl naturally assumed that since this was a book, of course it is read from right to left. Later I noticed the boy eyeballing a 14 year old girl from the same group. A small drama unfolded as he entreated his sister to go talk to her for him. She didn't want to, but he kept squeezing her hand and begging. Eventually she went to the other girl, and revealed her brother's affection for the girl. There was some excitement and embarrassment, and lots of seat swapping by the teenagers. Whether this girl was a first cousin, or a very distant cousin, or unrelated is not for me to say.

Suddenly, a 13 year old boy started wailing loudly. He was pointing at his head, and I was pleased to see that the old Chinese woman's vegetable bag which I had put up in the rack had been dripping muddy water the whole time. A pool of it had accumulated and splashed down all at once on the boy's head. They did another all-family verbal assault on her, and I grabbed her vegetables and placed them under my chair. She said "Xie xie," and the grand-father was laughing at the whole incident and pointing at the old woman and his grandson who got the muddy shower.

At Kashgar the Uighur family said goodbye and went off to sell their wares. Kashgar is a giant collection of adobe dwellings (or something like that) centered on a downtown core which includes a livestock trading market and a gigantic bazaar which sells just about everything. If it were smaller, and quainter, and located in a more modern part of the world, it would be a major tourist attraction. But what makes Kashgar interesting is precisely that it isn't a tourist attraction. It's a massive, fully functioning crossroads trading post which connects China, Pakistan, Afghanistan, Turkmenistan, Kyrgyzstan, and Uzbekistan. In addition, it serves as the cultural and religious center of Uighur life. In most of the neighborhoods of Kashgar, you find all of the Uighur men dressed like the grandfather from the train, and most of the women wearing burqas or hijabs. There are also Han Chinese neighborhoods and in the bazaar you see people from hundreds of different ethnic backgrounds representing the mosaic of ancient mountain tribal groups that is strung through Central Asia.

I stopped at a café in a Uighur neighborhood that was cooking some sort of meaty dumplings outdoors. I asked how much they cost, and the guy said 6 Chinese Yuan, which is about 50 US cents. I figured I would invest $2 and buy four. I tried to explain this to the guy, and he brought me inside the restaurant and asked me to sit down. I figured this was a ploy to get me to spend more money but it was so cold outside that I didn't care.

Inside the restaurant the best seats by the window with a view of the street were all free, and most of the customers were crammed together in the center of the room for some reason. I took a window seat. A waiter brought out some nice hot tea, then about 8 of the meat dumplings. I was still very chilly and I realized that there was a wood-fired stove with a pipe in the center of the room, and the reason everyone clustered there was for heat. I ate the delicious dumplings, asked for the bill, and it turned out that the price quote of 50 cents, which I had thought was the price of 1 dumpling, included 8 dumplings and the tea.

After lunch I explored the massive bazaar, and walked through most of the fascinating city of Kashgar. Then I caught a cab to the airport. My objective of reaching Kashgar by train having been achieved, I bought a 1 way plane ticket to Shanghai. The price was outrageously high, but I was too exhausted to even think about trekking across the Silk Road again. So even though I knew I was getting shanghaied I bought the ticket and flew in comfort back to the radically different world of luxurious, cosmopolitan Shanghai.

9 ENGLAND: WEST HAM UNITED

I drove my Euro-rental onto the ferry which connects Belgium to England. I parked the car and walked up to find the galley. I was hoping to load up on a last bit of continental cuisine before suffering the woes of British food. But the ferry only had overpriced sandwiches so I bought a coffee and took a seat at a cafeteria style table close to a window. A middle-aged couple from England named Mick and July sat down by me, and we started chatting.

Mick told me that they take vacations to Belgium mostly to pick up cheap cigarettes and beer at the duty free and then bring them back to England. Even after the cost of the ferry, he explained, they still come out ahead because they smoke and drink so much. "Speaking of drinking," he asked, "how about a pint?" He went to the galley and bought a round of two tasty English beers. "The wife's on the wagon," he told me. He winked at her and said, "…aren't you, love?" July told me a lot about life in Northern London while she worked on her knitting.

As we drank our pints, the Belgian Coast Guard conducted a practice rescue drill involving a man-overboard manikin, a helicopter, and a guy lowered into the water by a cable. Since we had nothing better to do this was pure entertainment, and people clapped at the end.

I got the next round of pints, and Mick asked me what stereotypes Americans have of the English. I said, "…highly educated and polite, with fantastic accents."

Mick scoffed at this and said, "No, that's just for the bloody upper class."

Then Mick made fun of the French for a while. He was on a roll, but was interrupted by some guy from across the room yelling something. We looked over and saw a Brit of about 20 staggering back and forth, and almost falling down due to the combined effects of alcohol, and the ferry rolling in the sea.

He pointed at Mick and yelled, "Fuckin'-A, mate!" He came towards us, still pointing at Mick yelling, "Yeeeeeeeeah, mate! Hammers! Fuckin'-ell'!" He fell down, spilled the beer he was holding, got back up and pressed on towards his objective, which seemed to be our table. "Oh, yeah!" he yelled, "Forever blowing bubbles, West Ham!" He made it to our table, tried to shake Mick's hand, but missed, and swept our drinks off the table and onto the floor. "Oh, bloody hell," he said, "West Ham!"

The Belgian ferry staff came over and hauled the guy away somewhere. After he was gone, there was an uncomfortable silence. "What was that all about?" I asked. July gave Mick a knowing look, and he showed me his forearm. It was a tattoo for the English football team, West Ham United.

"It's me team," he said, "The lad must be a fan as well. This happens to me a lot." July shook her head reproachfully. He rolled his eye, looked at me and said, "Well I can't take the bloody tattoo off, can I?" Then he looked defiantly at July and said, "And I don't want to either, love!" Mick flashed an evil grin and explained to me that, "West Ham is a special sort of football team. We have a reputation for, well ... smashing things up." I had never followed English football before meeting Mick, July and the drunken West Ham fan. So I decided at that moment to make West Ham United my favorite team.

Mick and July had planned to take a bus back to London so I offered them a ride. We got stuck in about 2 hours of heinous London Ring Road traffic, and eventually made it to their dingy, graffiti-laden apartment building, which was probably used in the filming of the movie, "A Clockwork Orange." When we pulled in, July asked if I would like to come up for a cup of tea. I don't really like tea, but I was dying to see a genuine Clockwork Orange council flat. "Council flat" in British English loosely translates to "The Projects" in American English. I accepted the tea offer.

As we got out of the car, Mick walked off somewhere by himself without saying goodbye or thank you for the ride. July said, "Oh, Mick's off to the pub." We walked up the stairs to her apartment which turned out to be filled with kids. They had the run of the place and the apartment was littered with crayons, dolls, candy wrappers, and curling irons. Somehow I had been transported from "A Clockwork Orange" to Monty Python's "Every Sperm is Precious" skit. The kids had millions of questions and demands for July. "Is daddy still in Belgium?" asked a 5 year old. "No love, he's at the pub."

A teenage girl said, "Oh dear, he's going to have a big headache tomorrow."

July said to the teenager, "Where are you going, dear?"

"Oh Suzy and I are going to take the tube into town."

"You're not wearin' that, are ya'?" asked July, referring to the girl's mini-skirt and cleavage-revealing top.

"Yeah, whah' of it?"

"You'll catch a bloody cold!"

"Oh, whah-eva!"

"Johnny," July said to a 9 year old boy, "Av' you eaten your broccoli yet?"

"No, mum" lamented the boy, "I don' like broccoli."

"Well, you've got to eat your broccoli unless you've got a belly-ache."

The boy thought for a minute and said, "Mummy, I've got a belly-ache."

"Oh, all right," said July. In the midst of all the domestic chaos, July still managed to brew me a giant cup of tea, and never once seemed flustered or overwhelmed by all the commotion.

I said, "In America, we call people like you 'Super-Mom'."

She smiled and said, "Actually only four of these kids are mine. Two of the little-uns' and two of the big-un's. The other five are all from other flats. They come over here cos' they know there's not so many rules". After tea, I thanked July and continued my journey.

10 JAPAN: SAMURAI DISCIPLINE; THE BUSINESSMEN

My Dad phoned me and said, "I've got good news and bad news: The good news is that Air Canada just called me and said I've won two round trip tickets to anywhere the airline flies. The bad news is that they expire 1 year after the award, and the award was apparently 50 weeks ago, but no one bothered to tell me."

"So in other words," I said, "We have 2 weeks to go anywhere Air Canada flies?"

"That's right."

"Wow. Other than Canada, where do they fly?"

"Let's see, they gave me a list … Germany, U.S.A., England, France, Japan, and a few other places."

"Hmmmm," I replied, "how about Japan?"

"Sounds good!"

"Domo Arigato!"

In a few days we landed in the overwhelming metropolis of Tokyo, Japan. We bought some Yen and caught a cab. The Japanese cabbie was about 50 years old and his car was equipped with about 17 blinking, high tech gadgets. "Listen to this," he said, as he cranked up his cutting edge sound system to full volume and rolled down the windows to make sure that all of Greater Tokyo's 32 million people could join us in listening to the Bon Jovi song "It's my Life." "Smoke?" he asked. We declined, and as he lit up a cigarette he said, "My wife tells me no smoking. Never. But you know what? IT'S MY LIFE!" He nodded his head triumphantly. "You guys want me to show you where to find beautiful Japanese ladies?"

"No thanks," I said, "We only date Canadian women."

"Ahhhhhh," he replied, "Very wise. Japanese women do not have proper breasts. Canadian women … proper breasts!"

After visiting The Emperor's Palace, we blew our daily budget on one beer in a bar, and some great sushi. Such are Tokyo's extremely high prices.

Since it was a short notice trip, we had no plan and the next day we were at a loss for where to go. We asked the hotel concierge for advice. He had a lot of suggestions about things like Kimono dress displays, traditional Japanese Kabuki Theater, origami classes, various other crafts, and visits to Buddhist monasteries. My Dad and I consulted and agreed that neither of us gave a shit about any of that stuff. We told the concierge that we were interested in hard core Japanese business and cheap beer. The savvy concierge recommended visiting The Tokyo Stock Exchange and a certain after work bar which he showed us on the map.

The Tokyo Stock Exchange was cool. It's a magnet for cash investments in some of the world's most innovative and powerful companies. The traders buzzed around the floor in an intense frenzy, and after the closing bell they all filed out to go to the after work bar which the concierge had recommended. The bar was filled with Japanese businessmen wearing suits which had the tie loosened by an inch and their top shirt buttons undone. That attire seems to be international business code for, "I just had the craziest work day of my life, and now I'm going to get rip-roaring drunk, so don't get in my way." Everybody was drinking Saki, smoking cigarettes, and yelling. There must have been 200 businessmen in the place, and I had my camera out because I figured that statistically, at least one of them should have a heart attack while we were there.

It was a nice night so we decided to get some relatively fresh Tokyo air and walk home. We noticed that every few blocks there was a vending machine selling cold, Japanese beer. Of all the high-tech, bizarre inventions we had seen while walking around Tokyo, these machines were certainly the most intriguing. We bought a few tall Sapporo beers which came in a silver can which was so cold, sleek, shiny, and artistic that we felt bad about throwing it away. We had considered bar hopping but the price at the beer machines was a fraction of the staggering pub prices, so we decided to see the great sights and flashing lights of Tokyo by night while strategically moving from vending machine to vending machine. After the Tokyo Tower, the Imperial Palace, the Meiji Shrine, and 7 or 8 vending machines we were in a deplorably drunk condition. A briefcase toting Japanese businessman even said "Gaijin" to us while walking by. Gaijin is a derogatory term which Japanese sometimes use to describe foreigners. It connotes sloppiness, lack of respect, public misbehavior, and bad discipline. All of these were qualities which my Dad and I fully displayed, so we laughed and thanked the man for his constructive criticism.

In order to continue with the business theme of the trip, the next day my Dad made a few phone calls back to North America. In spite of being unemployed and broke at the time, he somehow managed to line up a tour of an air conditioner factory, and a site visit to the Tokyo Electric Power Company (TEPCO).

The air conditioner factory was interesting but TEPCO was larger than life. Imagine one giant monster of a building, even bigger than Godzilla, which generates enough juice to power 40% of Tokyo. The building itself was a dizzying array of turbine engines, pipes, wires, and steel, all run by an army of guys wearing matching blue jump suits and white hard hats.

The monster was fed breakfast, lunch, and dinner by a giant ship which was filled with liquefied natural gas. (If you take natural gas and put it in a very cold fridge, it becomes a highly explosive liquid; and only takes up $1/600^{th}$ the space of normal natural gas). The ship was docked far off shore, and connected to the monster building by long umbilical cords which ran through the waters of Tokyo Harbor to reach the ship. Of course, the reason for docking the ship so far away was so that if some gaijin decided to drop his cigarette butt into the liquefied natural gas, the resulting massive explosion wouldn't wipe out all of Tokyo. (Only part of it).

All of this was explained to us in the conference room, where 12 somber executives and engineers were seated, ready to respond to our inquiries. Their leader gave us a long presentation about the role of TEPCO in Japanese society, and the technical specifications of the power plant itself. At the end of the show they inquired about our purpose in coming to TEPCO, and asked what further questions we had. Due to however my Dad lined up this tour, some guy's boss was told by someone else that a visiting business delegation was coming to see the plant. The guys in the conference room had no idea who we were, why we were there, or why they had to assemble 12 of their top men to meet us.

Naturally, we didn't want to respond with, "Well we won a free trip to Japan and we got bored of wandering around Tokyo drinking beer from vending machines." So we explained that we represented a North American Engineering firm whose name you wouldn't recognize because we were recently acquired by a large mining concern which in turn was a part of a global holding group. This convoluted response created enough confusion about our origin that none of the 12 men wanted to ask for clarification for fear of exposing his inability to follow what we had just said.

We then launched a series of hard questions about the capacity of such and such generator, or the use of different metallic alloys in the construction of various tubes. The men enjoyed answering these engineering questions which landed squarely in their comfort zone. Then I presented them with a framed black and white photo of Abraham Lincoln, and the conference wrapped up successfully. An engineer named Kazuki then gave us a great tour of the plant. At each point on the tour, Kazuki would loudly clap his hands twice, and at this signal one of the blue jump suit guys would run up, stand at attention like a soldier, and tell us about how his station operated.

When finished, Kazuki would clap his hands twice again; and the employee would run back to continue his work.

At one point, we boarded a Willy Wonka style tram to get from one part of the plant to the other. There was a comical American businessman on the tram who walked over and introduced himself to us. "Hey there, fellas! Mitch Maxwell, Schenectady, New York. I'm with General Electric. Been here 3 years now. Boy, I miss the heck outta' Schenectady." Mitch was fun to talk to and he had a lot of great info about how the power plant worked since he sold TEPCO their turbine generators. We were a bit worried that he would question us about our purpose, since it would be hard to bullshit this guy. Fortunately, he was a classic salesman who was constantly in "transmit" mode and rarely in "receive" mode. He talked non-stop and required little input from us.

When we were ready to leave TEPCO, Mitch said, "Listen guys, why don't you two and Kaz' come down to The American Club with me for dinner tonight? The wife'll be there and lemme' tell ya', The American Club makes the best damn T-bone steak in Tokyo. Comes with a great plate of fries, and after dinner we can hit the lounge for a Jack Daniels whiskey." We quickly said, "Sold!" and Mitch's driver took us all downtown to The American Club.

At the club, the food was fantastic, the whiskey was smooth, and Kazuki loosened his tie and undid his top button. He quickly changed from somber engineer to super-cool guy who had lots of funny stories about playing baseball as a kid in Japan. Mitch's wife was there and Kazuki's talk of baseball set her off on a rant and rave about the management of Little League Baseball in Schenectady.

By the end of the Tokyo trip we were flat broke, but no matter, because we were pretty much broke at the start of the trip as well. We had solved the problem of how to travel on a budget in Tokyo, one of the world's most expensive cities: win a free plane ticket, B.S. your way into factory tours and free dinners, and only drink beer from the vending machines.

11 JAPAN: SAMURAI DISCIPLINE; THE WARRIORS

Baggage claim in Tokyo was crowded with Americans. About half of the arriving passengers wore sharp crew cuts. The other half were strung out, wily dudes with hair down to their shoulders.

I was in the first group. We were American soldiers. Our mission in Japan was to practice the art of war with the Japanese Army. We were a mix of infantry officers, riflemen, gunners, and truckers.

The guys in the second group were American rockers. Their mission in Japan was to help Bon Jovi rock Asia. They were a mix of music executives, roadies, sound engineers, and truckers.

The baggage was slow in arriving so the soldiers and the rockers started talking to each other. Our truckers and their truckers had a lot in common so they got along well.

Their truckers learned that we were an Army battalion going to Hokkaido, which is the most Northern, remote, and conservative of Japan's four main islands. We would be close to the city of Sapporo, famous for the beer of the same name.

Our truckers learned that the New Jersey rock band Bon Jovi was just beginning a global concert tour, and these guys were the support team. They wanted to start the tour in a test market. (i.e., a place of no significance to the musical world where, if the concert really sucked, nobody would notice). Thus, the first city on the Bon Jovi tour was boring, snowy, Sapporo.

Our truckers said to their truckers, "Dude, we're going to the same shithole place in the middle of nowhere!" Word spread through the ranks of the musical troupe, and soon one of the music executives said to one of the infantry officers, "Hey, I made a few phone calls and Mr. Bon Jovi says he wants to have some American soldiers at the show. So we're going to hook you up with 100 tickets."

Once up in Hokkaido we immediately started to train with the Japanese Army. Our battalion, "The Wolfhounds," was from Hawaii, and Hokkaido was going through a series of freezing snow storms. The Japanese troops, who mostly grew up in Hokkaido, taught us a number of good tricks to help stay warm. On the shooting range we showed them some new machine gun sighting techniques, and demonstrated a relatively dangerous method of running a combat maneuvers exercise.

The Japanese soldiers were compelled to follow the regulations of their virtually weapons free society. This meant extreme measures were taken to ensure that no bullets were accidentally left behind on the range. Each Japanese soldier was followed by three safety inspectors. One inspector wore a bright red helmet, and his job was to tell the soldier when it was safe to start shooting. The second safety inspector wore a bright blue helmet, and his job was to pick up the casings of all the used bullets. The third safety inspector wore a bright white helmet, and his job was to make sure the first and second guys did their jobs. The soldiers themselves wore bright green helmets. So when 30 Japanese soldiers took the field at the same time, each followed by 3 safety inspectors, the result was 120 guys in bright red, blue, white, and green helmets running up the range. It was quite surreal and it looked as if a giant bag of M&M's had been spilled on Japan.

Later in the week, we did some mountain defense exercises. While our troops laughed at the M&M's display, the Japanese soldiers gained our respect in the mountains with masterful camouflage techniques, and a superior ability to move through the woods without being detected. There were many occasions when I looked at a bush as close as 10 feet away, and was surprised to find that it was actually a Japanese soldier who had used bushes, leaves, and face paint so well, that I couldn't distinguish him from his environment.

Another thing the Japanese were great at was bathing. Instead of showers, the Japanese had elaborate steam rooms where you sit on a stool, fill a bucket with hot water, pour it over yourself, lather up, and repeat. The floors were made of bamboo, and the décor was in traditional Japanese style. After the bucket room, you go to a large hot tub, and wade around for a while meditating.

After the bathing ritual and a sukiyaki dinner, I returned to the large tent which housed my platoon of 30 soldiers. Sergeant Steiger was on his cot reading. Sergeant Steiger was a tough, old infantryman from Massachusetts. He hated rich people, especially if they had a university education. He was a master in the art of sneaking around the woods, he was good at directing artillery fire, and the soldiers in his squad respected him.

Next to his cot, a group of 4 soldiers were playing cards, and beyond them was Private McRae, a short, fat, black kid of 18 from Georgia. Sergeant Steiger said, "McRae, what are you doing?"

"Nothin' Sergeant."

"You smell. Have you showered?"

"No, Sergeant."

"Why not? You're the only one in the squad who hasn't showered yet. If you want to go to the party with the Japanese tonight you have to shower. I don't need the whole Japanese Army saying that Sergeant Steiger's squad smells bad." McRae said ok, grabbed his towel, but then hesitated. "What's wrong McRae?"

"Sergeant, they got those weird Japanese showers."

"So?"

"Do I have to pour a bucket over my head?" Sergeant Steiger laughed out loud, which was rare, and sent McRae to the bucket room.

After McRae left, I asked, "Sergeant Steiger, what are you reading?" "Sir, it's just ...well...a book, sir."

"What book?"

Sergeant Steiger sheepishly looked at the floor and said, "Catcher in the Rye," sir.

"Cather in the fucking Rye?" I was shocked. "Sergeant Steiger, are you turning into an intellectual, on us?"

"No sir, it's just that, well..." he clearly wanted to change the subject, so I let him. "Sir, will we need to post guards for our weapons when we go to Bon Jovi tomorrow night?"

"No, tonight is the bender with the Japanese, and they are a heavy drinking culture. They are going to drink us under the table, and at least a few of our guys will lose control, cause trouble, and do something that deserves punishment. Their punishment can be to guard weapons while everyone else goes to Bon Jovi."

"Roger that, sir."

That night, we all boarded trucks and got carted over to a warehouse where the Japanese Battalion was waiting to meet us. Along the way we saw groups of protesters who wanted Japan to kick out all the U.S. soldiers. In some countries, protesters like this throw rotten fruits, yell "Yankee go home," and generally cause a ruckus. But true to Japanese manners, these protestors smiled at us, we waved, they waved back, and their signs simply said, "Please go home. Thank you."

At the warehouse, the Japanese had set up long tables with rows and rows of Saki, sushi, rice cakes, grilled meats, and cans of Sapporo beer. The Japanese soldiers were standing silently at the position of attention, and we lined up face to face with them. For a few minutes, the warehouse was just 1,000 stone faced soldiers from two nations separated only by Saki.

Then our commander gave the order, "Stand at, Ease." And instantly and silently every soldier snapped their hands behind their backs, moved their left boot one foot to the left and pointed their head in the direction of the commander. Admirably, the Japanese had learned our commands ahead of time. There were some solemn military rituals, flag raisings, and the observance of several serious Japanese and American traditions.

All this seemed to take an eternity since each soldier smelled the savory aroma of grilled meats, and saw the beads of icy water trickling down the cans of Sapporo. Our commander gave a speech and was followed by the Japanese commander, who made a rousing speech in Japanese. I had no idea what he was saying, but it sounded pretty cool. He ended his speech in English. "We welcome you, warriors of the powerful 27th Infantry Regiment! It is a great honor to train with you, powerful Wolfhounds! And now, we shall eat and drink together! I toast the 27th Infantry Regiment!" He raised a glass of Saki, yelled "Kampai!" and all of his soldiers yelled, "Kampai!" and drank their Saki.

The Americans caught on and started yelling "Kampai!" and drinking the Saki in front of them. The next few hours were about eating, drinking, and having fun with our new Japanese friends. There were occasional performances by Japanese and Americans who were probably originally destined to be musicians, but ended up in the Army by accident. One group of four soldiers did a hip hop quartet song that was remarkably professional. The Japanese gave them a standing ovation.

My counterpart was a Japanese Platoon Leader who was constantly ordering for more food and drink. He introduced me to an old man, his grandfather. Grandfather said he was a veteran of World War II, but assured us that his service was all on The Northern Manchurian Front fighting The Russians.

That night, the camp of tents was a zoo since every Japanese and American soldier was drunk and full of a sense of martial invincibility. One American soldier hit a Japanese officer in the face. Another destroyed the bamboo flooring in the bathing room. (These guys guarded our weapons the next night). A Japanese soldier stole a military jeep, and had a "Mr. Toad's Wild Ride" through the camp destroying everything in his path and driving over all of the tent ropes and stakes, thus causing the shelter of hundreds of soldiers to collapse on them in the middle of the night.

But in spite of the chaos we had made good friends with the Japanese and we invited them to take 50 of our Bon Jovi tickets. The next night, we bussed down to The Sapporo Dome, a massive and beautiful stadium, to see the inaugural sold out show of Bon Jovi's World Tour.

We met some girls inside the stadium while waiting in line for Yakitori, a skewered chicken snack. They were dressed like they were on their way to a church service, and when we quizzed them; they could only name one Bon Jovi Song, "It's My Life". (Of course). Inside the stadium something wasn't quite right. In spite of it being a sold out Bon Jovi show with 50,000 fans, it was deathly quiet, the smell of marijuana was noticeably absent, and not one of the girls showed us her tits. When the band came out, nobody cheered, but there was a strong, steady, 'Simon and Garfunkel Live' clap. Hokkaido was clearly devoid of the underground, spikey-haired, Japanese rock fanatics you find in Tokyo and Osaka.

After the first song, John Bon Jovi said, "how ya' guys doin'?!"

There was nothing but silence until a drunken soldier yelled, "We're three sheets to the wind on Japanese beer!"

Then Bon Jovi said, "How do I look?"

The same soldier yelled, "Like shit!!"

When Bon Jovi got to the popular songs, the normally docile crowd all held up glow-sticks and in unison did a cheesy 'everybody lean to the left, everybody lean to the right' move, well suited for a Britney Spears pop concert. At first this behavior was funny, but when the band played "Wanted," one of rock's most riveting and hard core anthems, this poppy glow-stick shit had to stop. Me and some other concerned citizens decided to do a lap around the stadium to raise awareness. We grabbed some Japanese soldiers to translate. We ran in front of large sections of fans and yelled, "Come on! This is mother-fuckin' rock concert! Time to get crazy! Bonzai!" At most sections, we just got the 'Simon and Garfunkel Live' clap, but at one section a lone-wolf Japanese rocker came jumping down over rows of docile fans yelling and screaming, and leaned down over the railing to give us high fives. If we can save just one ... it was all worth it.

After the crowd rallying work, we retreated to the concession stands for a beer and yakitori break. We expected there would be a long beer line of 40 people like most stadium events. But one of the advantages of seeing Bon Jovi in Hokkaido is that the good people stay in their seats during the performance, so the line was very short; two Canadians long, to be exact. These guys were teaching English in Japan and they entertained us with hysterical Northern wit while we drank our beers.

At the end of a normal rock concert, there is a massive jam of people trying to crowd through the exits at the same time, a process which can take half an hour. But at the Sapporo Dome, everybody sat motionless in their seats until an announcer on the loudspeaker said something in Japanese. One section of people stood up, while everybody else remained seated. Then another section was called up, and another until the stadium was cleared out. The whole exfiltration took about 8 minutes. Obviously, engineers had figured out the most efficient way to flow everybody out of the building. It was a genius innovation, and one which would probably only work in a place like Hokkaido where people actually follow the rules.

After the show we headed to our favorite Hokkaido bar for a night cap. This was a place we named "Nori's" after the owner, a sleepy eyed Japanese pot-head. His buddy Takahiro was always hanging out there. Takahiro worked by day in a potato chip factory and the bar usually had piles of his potato chips lying around. These chips were 100% natural and extra chunky so we would each usually down a few bags' worth, while drinking our beers. We probably went to that bar five times while were in Japan, and all five times, we were the only customers. A typical night involved us drinking Sapporo, Nori playing a Beastie Boys CD on repeat, and Nori and Takahiro disappearing for about ten minutes to smoke weed in the back room. After this, they would return and start devouring all the potato chips.

After the Bon Jovi concert, it was our last night out in Hokkaido and we figured we would go with the usual routine at Nori's bar. When we told him that we had just come from the big Bon Jovi concert, he pulled out a copy of Bon Jovi's best CD, "Slippery When Wet." So instead of the Beastie Boys on repeat, we had Bon Jovi on repeat. Thus, we wrapped up our Japan trip at Nori's bar eating healthy potato chips, drinking Sapporo, and rocking out to Bon Jovi in a glow-stick free environment.

12 U.S.A.: 24 HOURS IN MALIBU

Latigo Surf Break, Malibu, California; 8 a.m.:

I caught a decent wave, jumped up on my surfboard, and rode in close to the shore. After splashing through the last few feet of the Pacific Ocean, I sat refreshed on the beach for a few minutes to enjoy the moment. Behind some other surfers, I noticed a few dolphins jumping in and out of the water, and beyond them a sleek sailboat was gliding by.

I actually wasn't particularly good at surfing and for me to catch and ride a nice wave was a great way to start the day. I rinsed off, hit the hot tub in my building for about 10 minutes, and put on my work uniform. (This consisted of shorts, flip flops, a T-shirt, and sunglasses).

I drove in to Pepperdine University and took up my duties as pool life guard. My first task of the day was to monitor the pool during the girl's diving team practice. This consisted of watching 18-21 year old California girls spiral through the air in tight, one-piece bathing suits. I would occasionally flirt with them, but it was tough since Pepperdine University is a strict religious school and there is an excess of naïve innocence in the eyes of all the students.

One girl named Tina would talk with me a lot. I had bumped into her in the library once and we had coffee together afterwards. Today, she was trying out a dangerous, new dive. She pulled it off with grace and athleticism.

My partner life guard on the shift was a physics major named Mark. Mark was a hard core nerd who hated the sun. I tried to make him talk about physics to kill time, but he only wanted to talk about his favorite video game which was called War Craft. Towards the end of his shift, he would start nervously tapping his knee and mumbling things like, "Only 20 minutes until I'm inside with the air conditioning on, playing War Craft. C'mon. C'mon."

When Mark left he was replaced by Andy, a one dimensional jock from the water polo team. Most of the other lifeguards liked to talk just because the shift was so boring, but Andy would just stare straight ahead through his sunglasses at some spot on the other side of the pool. I tried to talk about a variety of topics with him; the weather, the girls on the diving team, Mexican food, War Craft, even the habits of the boss of the pool (a neurotic ex-tugboat Captain named Grady). But Andy was only capable of staring across the pool at the magic spot, politely nodding his head, and saying things like, "Yeah, I see what you mean," or "Yeah, definitely," or just, "Yeah".

Today was a particularly boring shift, so I decided to try one last topic on Andy, Water Polo. "Hey Andy, what's the penalty for a foul in water polo?" I asked.

"Oh," he replied, "If you foul someone, they get a 20-second one man advantage, during which time there is an 80% chance that they will score. And see, I'm a water polo goalie, so it's like, really bad when there's a foul. That's why if a coach has to choose between a guy who scores 6 goals per game but fouls a lot, or a guy who scores only 4 goals but never fouls, he's totally going to pick the 4 foul guy, 'cause I mean think about it for a second…" and he continued for 30 minutes on the subject of water polo while I just nodded my head and said, "Yeah, definitely." It was only mildly interesting, but now if I see a water polo game on TV I can follow what's going on, so at least I got something out of the conversation.

One of the most important rules which Grady the tug boat Captain laid down was that it was illegal to swim in lanes 11 through 15 during diving practice. Everybody knows it, and only an asshole would swim in lanes 11 through 15 during diving practice. And yet today some idiot was blatantly swimming laps in lane 13. We kept an ID on everyone at the lifeguard desk so before confronting him; I did a quick background check. Tina was walking by and I asked her, "Hey Tina, have you seen a 'Daniel Stern' at the pool during practice before? White male, above average height, curly hair, goofy face, and beady eyes?"

"Yeah, he's an actor. He was in that movie Home Alone as a burglar or drug dealer or something." So apparently this guy had a history of criminal activity, which explained his willingness to swim in lane 13.

I walked over to him and said, "Excuse me, sir; regulations prohibit swimming in lanes 11 through 15 during diving practice. Please move to lane 10, or less." He looked confused and disappointed.

"But Grady lets me swim in Lane 13 during diving practice." "Well Grady's not here right now. Please move to lane 10 or less, it's for your safety."

"Ahhh, ok," he said, and he swam down to lane 10.

When he left the pool and picked up his ID he was very polite and cool to everybody, in contrast to many of the richos from Malibu who pay to use the pool and become very rude and obnoxious anytime they have to obey pool rules. (The Pepperdine University pool tends to attract a lot of wealth and Hollywood star power).

As I pondered the incident, I realized two things: #1. This was the only case I had ever seen where Grady made even the slightest exception to the rules and regulations of his pool. Therefore, Grady, in spite of his image as a salty dog veteran of the shipping industry, is just as bedazzled by Hollywood movie stars as every other moron in this city and probably would sell his soul to get a photo with a third rate, no name actor like Daniel Stern.

#2, in spite of my image as a laid back Californian who is all about good vibrations, I had been a complete asshole to Mr. Stearn. This was the only case in which I had used a forceful policeman voice on a customer of the pool. I could have just as easily said, "Hey dude; is it cool if you just move down a few lanes while diving practice is on? Sorry to interrupt your swim, looks like you're doin' some serious laps, bro!" Therefore, I was overreacting in response to my disgust with the cult worship of Hollywood actors; a group of professionals who I consider to be hired clowns for the idiot masses.

To be honest, this feeling was accentuated when my ex-girlfriend told me how she was swimming in the Pepperdine pool one day and at the end of a lap she looked up to see the sun-tanned, physically fit figure of Pierce Brosnan (aka James Bond) staring down at her wearing nothing but a Speedo. He asked her with a charming British accent, "Pardon me, may I share your lane with you?" She agreed, and had a good swim session with Mr. Double-0-fucking-7. She also remarked, "So sad, but it could never work between me and him, I'm too young." Whatever.

All of these deep thoughts kept me occupied until 20 minutes before the end of my shift. I started tapping my knee and mumbling, "20 minutes until I'm back at my apartment. C'mon. C'mon."

My Apartment; 4 p.m.:

Marie was waiting when I got back. She was La Belle femme de France and she had volunteered to help me get ready for a BBQ party I was hosting that evening. After setting up the BBQ, the volleyball net, the bar down by the beach, and the inflatable gnome, we took a break. She had a glass of wine, and I had a glass of water with a couple of ice cubes. She looked at my drink and said, "How can you drink that stuff, it's not healthy."

"It's water."

"You mean water WITH ice cubes!"

I looked at my glass of ice water in shock and asked, "Ice cubes cause cancer?"

"Oh, so funny." she growled, "No. It's not natural for your body to consume something so cold, and it has to work overtime to heat everything up. It's bad for you!"

"Well, I like living on the edge."

Then she said in French, "You Americans are crazy."

The guests arrived, about 30 in all, and they consumed BBQ'ed burgers, cold beer, French cheese, and ice water. We played some volleyball, splashed in the surf, and watched a particularly gorgeous sunset.

One of the guests thought it was necessary to bring a lot of Malibu Rum since we were in Malibu. He broke out many bottles of it at sun down, and the guests started getting pretty liquored up. Another guy declared himself DJ, and soon he had all the girls dancing on the volleyball court in bikinis. The DJ was so good that even the 2 German guys, Max and Günther, were dancing.

Soon it was pool time. I asked a blonde girl named Tracy to lead the crowd up to the pool. Tracy was a former Olympic Skiing aspirant, and an intern for Vice President Dick Cheney. "Tracy, please make sure they jump into the cold pool first, and then the hot tub, otherwise they won't get the full effect," I said. Meanwhile, Herr Max und Herr Günther helped me clean up the BBQ area.

"Are you Deutschlanders having fun?" I asked

"Ja, said Günther, in a thick Bavarian accent. I was doing zee dirty dancing with a hot girl from zee tennis team."

After the cleanup Günther said, "Time for zee Germans to do zee ocean svim." Max and Günther started sprinting towards the ocean. I was covered in BBQ grease and empty beer can residue, so I figured I would join them for the swim and rinse it off. We crashed into the waves and swam quickly out about 200 feet. The water was frosty but it was exhilarating. We howled at the moon, and to our surprise, our howls were answered by female voices from a seaside beach mansion one cove down from where we were swimming. Some girls on a balcony were waving us over so we swam towards them with alacrity and dispatch.

We rushed out of the water onto the beach in front of the mansion and found that our path to the girls was blocked by a small rise of coastal rocks on top of which the mansion was built. One of the girls yelled in a Texas accent, "If ya'll want to see us, ya'll need to climb on up!" We were shivering wet from the cold ocean water and only wearing bathing suits, but we scaled the rocks and climbed onto the mansion's balcony. The girls cheered and rewarded us with Coor's Light beers, and said, "Welcome to our white trash party!" I looked around the room and noticed a lot of daisy dukes, race car hats, and a shrine to Dale Earnhardt, Sr., 1951-2001, with candles lit, a model #3 race car, and a photo of the legend himself. Max, who back in Germany was into car racing, beer, and watching sports, seemed to feel a deep connection to these people. He pointed to the Dale Earnhardt, Sr. shrine and said, "Das ist gut."

A big ol' fella sporting a ZZ Top beard and some cheap sunglasses overheard this strange German tongue and said, "ya'll aren't from these parts are ya'?"

The girls dried us off and fed us chips with ranch dressing and pop tarts. After partying with these people for a while, I couldn't be sure whether we were at a white trash theme party, or an actual white trash party. I was about to investigate, but I was interrupted by someone yelling urgently form from the beach below. It was another German friend of ours, Frau Sylvia. "Greg, you must come quickly, there is a problem with zee party!"

We thanked the red necks, said goodbye to Mr. Earnhardt, and climbed back down the rocks. We sprinted up the beach to my apartment to find out what the problem was. By the time we got back, the problem had been solved. Apparently, one of the neighbors had complained loudly that there were empty vodka bottles broken on the stairs, people were behaving inappropriately in the hot tub, and that the noise of the party was unbearable.

Building Security came to shut the party down, but Tracy, the Dick Cheney aid, issued a statement which denied our involvement with either the hot tub affair, or the vodka bottle incident. She conceded that we were making too much noise and offered an apology on behalf of the party as a whole. Security backed down and the party continued.

It was nice to see that security was enlightened enough to understand that the neighbor's request to stop the party was unreasonable, as are <u>all</u> requests by a neighbor to stop a good party. Think about it; is there any major value system, be it Judeo-Christian, Buddhist, Utilitarian, or Confucian, in which the happiness of one individual (in this case the neighbor) is valued more highly than the happiness of 30 other human beings?

When I entered my apartment it was crowded with drunken revelers and lots of people were dancing and doing rum shots. When the Huns and I entered, people stopped what they were doing and shouted, "Oh, my God! You're back! Where were you? Security came! We thought you had drowned!"

"So," replied Max, "You are saying that you thought we had drowned and yet this didn't stop you from drinking and doing zee dancing?" The crowd saw his point, said sorry, and brought out more rum.

Tracy then proposed a toast which everybody blindly repeated, "To Dick!" "To Dick!"

About two hours later I got a call from my friend Rick who came to the party but had disappeared for 3 hours. "Hey man, we're stuck at the gate! We can't get into your building."

"Who is 'we'?" I asked.

"Oh, me and Anna from Canada."

"Ok, I'll come down and let you in." At the gate, Anna and Rick were giggling wildly and cuddling. I found out later that they had gotten stuck outside the gate together, and the reason it took Rick three hours to implement the simple solution of calling me is that he and Anna spent three hours making out and falling in love.

They spent the rest of the night lying together on the living room carpet in front of the fake 70's fireplace, wearing turtle necks, and drinking cheap chardonnay. The incident at the gate ultimately led to Anna and Rick getting married.

At about 1 a.m., I wrapped up the party; it had been a good one. As I was escorting people through the hall, I noticed that there were several other parties going on. After my group had left, I hit the hot tub to relax after all the work of hosting. The hot tub was filled with people from the other parties including a few hotties from the university. I jumped into the hot tub and heard a drunk girl's voice behind me say, "Oh my God, is that you, Greg?!" It was Tina, the innocent diver. She was in jeans and a t-shirt and lamented that she couldn't get into the hot tub because she forgot her bathing suit.

Jokingly, I said, "Yeah, when that happens to me, I just swim in my underwear." She took the suggestion seriously and soon she was in the hot tub wearing just a turquoise bra and matching thong panties.

One of her friends said, "I can't believe we ran out of alcohol, we are like, such dumb undergrads." I still had 20 types of booze left over from my party, and in no time I hooked up everyone in the hot tub with an appropriate beverage.

Tina asked if she could use my bathroom, and walked off to my apartment. Meanwhile, a cool neighbor of mine named Marcos showed up. He was an Argentinian aristocrat whose parents sent him to Pepperdine since, as a religious school, it would protect him from vice.

Marcos jumped into the hot tub and I handed him a rum and coke. "Gregorio," he said, "I am high as a fuckin' kite." His girlfriend, a mid-Westerner who was on the women's basketball team, came and sat on his lap in the hot tub. I had seen her a lot in her basketball uniform and always thought she was kind of ugly. But in a bikini in a hot tub with steam rising up behind her she looked more like a swimsuit model. Beauty all depends on the environment.

"So did you hear about Andy?" asked Marcos.

"Andy the water polo player?" asked his girlfriend.

"Yeah," said Marcos, "I saw him stumbling up the stairs a few hours ago with a bottle of vodka in his hand and some fine chica under his arm. She started kissing him, he dropped the bottle and it smashed all over the stairs. Then I heard they went to the hot tub and made love in the moonlight. So beautiful … what passion. Man, I am soooooo hungry. Gregorio, let's get some food and go to the after party."

"What after party?" I asked.

"Just trust me. You have to come." I had a plate of leftover BBQ'ed burgers so a group of us walked back to my apartment. The door was wide open. We walked in and found Tina in my kitchen happily singing a song to herself, and devouring the hamburgers. She had eaten exactly half of each hamburger. There was also a box of Cap'n Crunch cereal tipped over and the cereal was spilled all over the floor. "Oh, hi Greg," she said, "Your Cap'n Crunch is delicious. And there were some potato chips around here somewhere but I don't know what happened to them." Marcos and his girlfriend ate the other halves of the burgers and then one of the Pepperdine girls remembered that they had to be back in time for curfew or something like that. We drove them home and had to talk our way through security because it was past their bedtime. The girls said goodnight and then a group of us drove into the Malibu Hills to find the after party.

A vacant lot in the Malibu Hills; 4 a.m.:

About 200 people were doing strange gypsy dances and fondling each other. This after-party was a bizarre collection of people and the average age was about 40. (Roughly double that of the hot tub party). About 20% of the crowd was dressed in Grateful Dead hippie outfits, and they looked relatively conservative compared to the rest of the group. One woman was wearing a ridiculous, bright red spandex body suit which stretched from ankles to shoulders. She was about 42, and blessed with an incredibly sexy body and a 1970's disco groupie appeal. She caught my eye and yelled, "Oh my god! It's you!"

I said, "Yeah, it's me!" even though I had no idea who she was.

"Wow, how was Scotland?!"

"Oh, it was just … crazy."

"Crazy? No way!"

"Yeah, crazy cold!"

I don't know where she got Scotland from, and just then two police cars stormed up to the vacant lot. The girl took flight, and the cops shut the party down. Surprisingly, the crowd complied very quickly, packed up all of the music and lighting equipment they had set up, and moved off in an orderly fashion.

Then the police left, and as soon as they were gone, the whole crowd simply moved to a big house that was right across the street. Apparently, this was a planned maneuver. It worked, and the party continued inside the house. There was a troupe of conga drummers playing and people dancing in various rooms. A cash bar was set up in the courtyard, and people were draped all over the stairs. The red one reappeared and danced to the conga drums with me for a while. She told me that this whole party was actually a reunion for a large group which had travelled together to the annual "Burning

Man" festival. (Burning Man is a desert gathering for hedonists and pagans, at which a giant effigy of a man is burned).

Soon the sun was up and Marcos, his girlfriend and I decided to head home. I was clean sober so I volunteered to be the driver. As I was unlocking the door, I saw a flash of red out of the corner of my eye. "Hey, Mr. Scotland!" said spandex woman, "You can't run away without saying goodbye! Do you get out to the valley much? You should call me, we haven't partied together since Burning Man, baby!" She gave me a sheet of paper that said "Stacey: 818-555-3619." Then she gave me a voluptuous, full bodied hug and I couldn't resist giving her a double handed squeeze on the ass. She giggled and swallowed my ear. Then she sauntered back to the party swinging her hips left and right, and pointing one hand up into the sky she yelled, "Malibuuuuuuuu!"

I got back to my apartment and heard the muffled sound of a Justin Timberlake song playing. (Something which would never happen in my home under normal conditions). I was so tired, I ignored it, but then I heard it again and realized it was a cell phone ringing. I followed the sound to a mysterious backpack which was hidden behind my couch. Out of curiosity, I answered it. "Hello?"

"Hi, who is this?" said a girl's voice.

"You called me, who are you?"

"Oh, sorry, it's Tina, I lost my cell phone and I'm calling it."

"Oh, this is Greg, your phone, and I guess your backpack, are in my apartment."

"Weird," she said. "Where is your apartment?"

Pepperdine University Dorm; 8 a.m.:

After clearing up the confusion, I drove over to the university to give Tina her bag and phone. She looked uncomfortably hung over and clearly didn't remember the night before. She asked, "So … was I really obnoxious last night?"

"No, you were cool. Everybody just partied for a while then went home."

"Oh, thanks. Well, I need to go sleep now, but we should have coffee again soon, ok?"

"Yeah, that would be awesome."

I drove home exhausted, and found my apartment was littered with debris from the night's festivities. I brushed my teeth, tripped over an empty bottle of Malibu rum, and crashed onto my bed.

13 AFGHANISTAN: THE CANUCKS

Some Norwegian commandos and I spent the day down at the Tarnak Farms range shooting old Soviet tanks and helicopters. The range was a short ride from Kandahar Airfield, and right next door to the Taliban Barracks, formerly home to perhaps 600 of the Taliban's fighters. This barracks had been smashed a few months earlier by a U.S. Air Force bomb, and was now essentially a grave yard.

The range was littered with relics from the Soviet invasion of Afghanistan in the 1980's. Dead helicopters, planes, and tanks had been rusting there for two decades. These ghostly dinosaurs were once powerful military machines operated by guys just like me.

The Norwegians had crates and crates of extra machine gun ammunition and anti-tank rockets. I had made friends with them and they were nice enough to invite me to try out their hardware. After a few hours of target practice we walked off the range, careful to watch out for mines and unexploded bomblets. A couple weeks before, a Navy Seal had accidentally stepped on a mine on this range and it blew his foot off.

Later that day, I met up with a Major from a newly arrived Canadian unit, "Princess Patricia's Canadian Light Infantry". (Aka "The Picklies") We talked business for a while and then B.S.'ed about the coming Olympic hockey tournament. (...which Canada ended up winning decisively)

The Picklies were instantly popular with other troops on the base since they were the first soldiers in Afghanistan to bring certain essential tools for running a good war: port-a-potties and a suction truck to clean them out. More importantly, they brought "Coyotes" a Canadian armored recon vehicle, thus providing mobile ground firepower, something we sorely lacked before the Canadians arrived.

The Picklies quickly earned a reputation for being competent, no bull-shit soldiers. They worked hard, never complained, and were eager to take on combat missions.

A few nights after my trip to the range, I had an all night shift "clearing fires". This basically meant keeping track of where all the soldiers in my unit were, and before a bomb was dropped anywhere in Afghanistan, making sure that none of our troops were under it. So I sat in a room full of maps and radios and listened to an eerie stream of reports and chatter signifying bombs dropped, helicopters crashed, mines hit, enemy killed, wounded soldiers evacuated, etc.

My group was a bizarre mix of troops from 7 allied countries including Canada, and they were spread in small teams all across Afghanistan. I knew every Afghan province by heart, and kept firm tabs on where each team was and what it was doing. Sometimes there would be action in 5 spots at once, and sometimes it would be dead silent for 5 or 6 hours at a time. One night, nothing out of the ordinary had happened for many hours. Then suddenly there was a thunderous explosion somewhere and the building I was in shook and rocked like it was an earthquake. "What the fuck was that?" I thought. I called each of the staff officers from the various countries and told them to count all their people, confirm their safety, and report back. They were all awake and alert thanks to the explosion, and they reported back very quickly that all were safe.

Then I got a call from my next higher headquarters asking me "Are all your Canadians inside the wire?"

"Roger," I replied "just checked."

"Check again, there have been Canadian casualties". I called back to the Canadian officer, relayed the news, and told him to double check his men. He checked, called back, and said, "We're all inside the wire, maybe it was the Picklies." "Yeah, maybe," I replied. My Canadians weren't part of the Picklies, and I reported back to my headquarters that our Canadians were all safe.

I remembered the Canadian Major from the Picklies mentioning that his troops would be shooting on the range that night. Knowing how dangerous the range was I thought perhaps the Canadians had set off a mine, but no mine would make that large an explosion.

Later, we learned what had happened. The Canadians had been shooting on the range, and as always when shooting at night, some of the tracers deflected up into the air. A U.S. Air Force F-16 jet happened to be flying by at that time, and mistook the upward moving tracer fire to be enemy shooting at him. So he bombed the location to destroy what he thought to be enemy anti-aircraft fire.

Four Canadian soldiers were killed, and eight seriously wounded by the exploding bomb on the range that night. Private Richard Green, Private

Nathan Smith, Corporal Ainsworth Dyer, and Sergeant Marc Léger, may you rest in peace. They were the first Canadians killed in the war.

The Picklies, to their credit, continued their mission with the same energy and spirit of team work as before. They understood that such tragedies are bound to occur every so often in war if you want to have the benefits of an Air Force (for example, eliminating 600 Taliban fighters in their barracks without the loss of a single friendly soldier. 600 Taliban fighters would certainly have killed more than 4 allied soldiers).

The pilot will surely feel guilty for the rest of his life, and will constantly regret the decision he made on that night. It's very easy for me to say that he should have waited through the process of clearing fires to confirm that he was not bombing friendly troops. But he was under the impression that he was being fired at, and that he needed to react quickly to protect himself.

Soon after the incident, a moving memorial service was held for the troops. Soldiers from seven different countries were in attendance. I had seen a few of these for American troops, but for most of the young Canadian soldiers, this was the first time they had lost a comrade. Each of the four soldiers had a speech given for him by one of his squad mates. The first three were younger soldiers and they spoke at length about what the guys were like. As only Canadians can do, they each threw a few lines of hysterical wit into their otherwise somber and respectful speeches, reducing many of the soldiers watching to either tears of sadness or tears of laughter.

The last speech was for the oldest casualty, Sergeant Marc Léger. He was a vet of Canada's peacekeeping operations in the Balkans. The soldier giving the speech talked about how in the Balkans Sergeant Léger was a Squad Leader in charge of a small village which had been ravaged by the violence in the Balkans. Sergeant Léger developed a great relationship with the people in the village, and did a superb job of keeping the peace, and helping the village rebuild itself. The locals loved him and nicknamed him King Marc. King Marc's soldiers kept the nickname alive after he returned to Canada. Then King Marc put his heart and soul into getting the soldiers of his squad ready to fight in Afghanistan. The speaker related several examples of King Marc's work in Afghanistan, and he also spoke of the family King Marc left behind in Canada. Finally, the speaker concluded with a Shakespeare quote: "The King is dead. Long live the King!"

14 AFGHANISTAN: THE VIKINGS

The Norwegian Special Operations Forces had cool uniforms and rolled around the camp on tricked-out' off-road motorbikes. They had been designed as a long range reconnaissance force whose mission in the 80's was to watch for Soviet Forces attacking Europe. They were convinced that underground criminal organizations would buy and sell their names and identities if they had the chance, so they only used fake names. George, their leader, was a tough old bastard of about 45 who only spoke Norwegian. This was surprising since most people in Norway speak better English than Americans. But it also gave him a super-patriot Norgiest-of-The-Norwegians appeal, which was good for him to have as Commander.

Robert, their chief staff officer was my counterpart. He was a very cool guy of about 28 who would go out of his way to help the other countries in our camp. For example, when some of our troops went on a mission to a part of Afghanistan for which we lacked adequate maps, he had his maps guy somehow get ahold of some old maps made by the Soviets in 86'. And since Afghanistan only builds a new building about once every 300 years, these maps were reasonably accurate.

The rafters in our three-story-high helicopter hanger were littered with twisted metal and broken sheets of glass due to an air strike we had hit it with 3 months prior. So it was dangerous to work inside that building. Robert generously volunteered one of his mountain warfare experts to clear the rafters out. This guy motor-biked over to the hanger, pulled some high tech climbing ropes and clips out of his backpack, and proceeded to crawl around the rafters like Spiderman, throwing down any potentially dangerous debris.

And Robert always shared his supply of beef jerky with me which came in a bag that said "Smoke Craft Beef Jerky: For Bold Americans".

Soon, Headquarters had assigned a deep reconnaissance mission to the Norwegians, who we all called "The Vikings." They were to infiltrate into Northeast Afghanistan by helicopter and recon the border crossings over the mountains in between Afghanistan and Pakistan. The night before their departure, they had a pre-combat party and invited all the other soldiers from the different countries in our group. Their mission would take them to a very dangerous part of Afghanistan and it was quite possible that for some of them this would be their last party.

That morning, The Vikings had received a plane load of machine gun ammunition and grenades for use on the coming mission. There was lots of extra space on the plane, so they loaded pallets full of Scandinavian vodka and fresh shrimp from the fjords of Norway. They also constructed a large jacuzzi made from wood, plastic sheets and a tube connected to an air pump which made bubbles. Last, some of The Vikings, (who were mostly red necks from Norway's far north), had procured a large camel, killed it, skinned it, and slowly roasted it to create a succulent meat dish.

Robert broke out an acoustic guitar and the party, about 200 soldiers in all, clapped along as he sang some great alternative rock tunes. I hit the hot tub after some shrimp, camel, and vodka.

After his gig, Robert jumped in the hot tub and said he had some bad news. "Greg, we have an issue with the locations we have been assigned to watch on the border."

"What's wrong?" I asked.

"Well, the assholes at Headquarters gave as a 10 kilometer sector to watch, which is fine, but then they marked out about 8 border crossing positions for us to monitor. If you look at a map of that region closely, you can see that these positions are not all necessary."

"Ansfrid, bring me a map," he called to a soldier. Then he corrected himself, "Bob, bring me a map." Bob brought a map over and held it out next to the hot tub. "So," Robert explained, "these 8 points are where the trails cross from Pakistan over the border into Afghanistan."

"Ok."

"Well, the trails are surrounded by giant mountains which can't be crossed. And if you follow these trails on the map back into Afghanistan, you can see that many of them connect." Where Robert was pointing you could see a fork in the road where the fork tongs went to Pakistan and the fork handle went to Afghanistan.

"I see," I said, "So why not recon at that spot or behind it somewhere on the handle and one team can do the job of two?"

"Exactly!" yelled Robert. "And yet these assholes at Headquarters are making us watch 8 spots when we could really watch perhaps only 4. And with fewer spots our guys could either beef up security, or get more sleep, and be able to last longer. So what the fuck?!" The logic made perfect sense.

"Don't worry, Robert", I said, "The guy who marked those 8 positions has 100 kilometers of border and 80 positions to worry about, and the reason he sent them down to you early is so you could check em' out and give feedback. I'll call him up and get the positions changed ASAP. Plus we'll re-task the landing zones for the helo's and make sure the resupply and evacuation plan is modified. The whole process will take about 40 minutes."

"Sounds great," said Robert. "Now where did that shrimp tray go?"

About 6 hours later, the camel had been devoured, the shrimp and vodka were depleted, the hot tub had been drained, and The Vikings were geared up in battle armor and moving towards the airfield ready to fly into combat.

15 AFGHANISTAN: THE KIWIS

EXCERPT FROM OPERATIONAL SUMMARY #146, NEW ZEALAND FORCES, AFGHANISTAN:

"…this Afghan bloke was looking suspicious and eyeing our position. We drove in his direction to question him. We fired a couple warning shots at him but for some reason he kept running. Then, a right royal chase ensued! We ran him down and detained him. We questioned him and he claimed to be a local salesman of imported goods. Given his appearance, he was probably selling goods on the sham. (Black market). Based on an inspection of his teeth we concluded that he must have spent some time out of the country to get such high quality dental work. He confessed to having spent 7 years in Iran, supposedly for a construction job.

Later in the day we conducted check point operations and searched more than 100 vehicles. In one vehicle we found a farmer hauling a huge supply of opium. We confiscated the farmer's opium. This seemed to seriously upset him. He said it was a whole season's crop. We told him we understood that he was just a poor farmer trying to make a living and gave him his opium back … in return for the name and location of the market where opium is traded in Kandahar City."

The Kiwis (i.e., the guys from New Zealand) had spent the last month tearing through Kandahar and Helmand provinces in 9 Hummer jeeps. The bearded blokes mounted .50 cals (very heavy machine guns), SAWs (light machine guns), and mark 19's (automatic grenade launchers) on the jeeps, drove into Indian country, and looked for a fight. To their dismay the bad guys had enough sense not to try anything silly while this patrol was on the move. However, they managed to capture a good haul of relatively important prisoners, collected valuable intelligence, and generally sent a message that the Taliban was not in charge out there.

Now they were back in Kandahar for a 6 day rest, before going back on the prowl for another month. They spent their 6 day break reloading on ammunition, getting some sleep, fixing their jeeps, and drinking beer. They even found time to celebrate their national holiday, ANZAC day, and invited all of us to join them.

On this day of national celebration the Kiwis celebrate what amounts to the birth of their nation as a separate entity from The United Kingdom. Unfortunately, this was a painful birth which required thousands of Kiwis and Aussies to fall prey to Turkish machine guns and incompetent British generalship on the beaches of Gallipoli during World War I. I once asked a British Major how he felt about Britain's penchant for using troops from its colonies as cannon fodder in war. He replied, "Well young man, if you can't use them as cannon fodder, what's the point of having colonies?" We actually had a Turkish Officer assigned to us for a while. However, he was reassigned to Kabul before Anzac day. (Perhaps for his safety).

Anzac day wound up being a raucous event. It started with a terrifying Haka war dance, similar to that which precedes a New Zealand rugby game. Then there was a moving ceremony in honor of fallen soldiers, along with a brief history of New Zealand. They had displays set up about New Zealand and a chaplain gave a fiery sermon that was full of warrior spirit and biblical violence. We then ate some Afghan grub and proceeded to "The Pilly-Grim" which was the Kiwis' homemade bar. After barbequed chicken and a bonfire, everyone "got on the piss" (i.e. drank beer), and some of the Kiwis decided to test their strength by driving a large, rusty drill bit through a thick wooden table by hand.

Some Germans arrived, (who the Kiwis referred to as "The Nazis") and I got into it with them over who was going to win the upcoming World Cup Soccer game between Germany and the U.S. Of course I fully expected the U.S. to get crushed but it was enough to get a rise out of them. Overhearing this conversation, the Kiwis made sure we understood that the real World Cup was in rugby and that New Zealand was going to win it.

A Danish C-130 (cargo plane) had been grounded for maintenance problems in Kandahar so their crew crashed the Kiwi party. These guys were older and fatter than most legitimate military organizations and they earned their keep by telling enticing stories of beautiful women in the discos of Bishkek, Kyrgyzstan where they were temporarily based. Isn't every man's dream-girl a Kyrgyz babe from Bishkek? Somehow the presence of the Danes got the Kiwis to start making fun of the French, and this carried the conversation for about 20 minutes.

After a good night of revelry, I noticed the Kiwi jeep commander looking drunk and miserable. He was the kind of guy who was happiest when he was in combat. "What's wrong, mate?" I asked.

He replied, "Kandahar…shit. I'm still only in Kandahar."

16 AFGHANISTAN: CITY OF KANDAHAR

Kandahar, Afghanistan, 4 months after 9/11: Just came off a 12 hour night shift. 0600. Ready for sleep. Major Haywood asks, "Ready to go on patrol with the Green Berets?"

"Roger".

"Meet 0930 in the tactical operations center." I prep my equipment, clean my assault rifle, and borrow a grenade.

A Lieutenant Colonel, an intelligence officer from New Zealand, and I, meet with the Green Berets. They brief the route into town. If we make enemy contact before this point, we return to base. Calls signs, medical plan etc. 1 Toyota SUV, one Toyota pick-up truck. One man rides in the back of the pick-up. He is there for rear security plus mobility in the event of a firefight.

The Green Berets are all bearded and wearing civilian clothes. Everyone's got bullet proof vests, weapons, and ammo. Lock and load our assault rifles as we exit the camp perimeter. Wave to local friendly Afghan Military Forces (AMF) as we pass the Afghan gate.

Drive on highway 4, the main road between Pakistan and Kandahar. 2 lanes are paved. Future New York City cab drivers are in every car. We pass several adobe enclaves. Through a pass between two ridges, we see the city of Kandahar in the distance. Stunning brown, rocky mountains rise out of the desert. On the outskirts of town eight foot by eight foot shacks line the road. Afghans in the stalls are selling various third world riff raff. Traders of Pakistani goods, most likely. Everyone stares at us, and many wave. It feels like we're on the great Lahore road of Rudyard Kipling fame even though that's a couple hundred kilometers away. People walk, drive cars, ride bikes and donkeys…they all make the great trek.

A drive-in pit of muddy water serves as the car wash. Shacks turn into two-story ratty structures as we get closer to the center of town. The population grows. Near the center of the city we're on a boulevard with the occasional 3-story building, lots of mosques, gates, and interesting architecture. Central Asian glory. Hustle and bustle. Sandals, robes, cylindrical hats, and beards are in this season.

We arrive at the Governor's palace. It's run down but still justifies the term palace. AMF soldiers guard the entryway. We pull through the gates and enter the safe-house. We unload our guns. Inside the building I smell dried up red wine that was probably spilled on the carpet a week ago. The New Zealand intelligence officer and the Green Berets in the safe-house exchange information about where they are going to operate. We go "next door". "Next door" is where the CIA guys hang out. A man from the CIA briefs us on a Brigade of Afghans which is run by a bad guy but the Brigade technically belongs to the legitimate Afghan Government. (So we can't kill them). The CIA guy is condescending and annoying. He admits, though, that the Green Berets have a better ground picture from actually being outside the wire on a daily basis and working with AMF a lot.

The rooftop view of Kandahar is fantastic. The Governor's Palace is the tallest building in the city (four stories) so we can see everything. This is a true old-world Islamic city. Other than some cars and a few Coca-Cola ads, this is probably about how the city looked in the 9th Century when Islam first became the leading religion of Afghanistan. The view is fascinating and I could stare at it for hours. The busy market street grows from out of the palace. There are some parks with many wanderers. Adobe town houses are packed tight in the center of the city. There are a few three-story concrete attempts at buildings adjacent to the central market place. Minarets dot the skyline of Kandahar, like steeples used to serve the skylines of old European towns. A random multi-story building springs up here and there about one kilometer away. A few smoke stacks rise out of adobe buildings which appear to be small brick factories or kilns. Farther out are somewhat larger adobe bungalows with fortress-like walls. The color of these buildings matches the desert and they blend right into the hills.

Small mountains ring the city far beyond its limits. They are sedate and worthy of sun beaten worship. Bicycles jingle, people talk or yell in Pashtu, and Arabesque music blares on a primitive speaker so the whole downtown can groove to it. You can feel and hear the hum of this active town, a trading gateway between Pakistan and Southern Afghanistan.

The roof of the palace is lined with sand bags. Anti-tank rockets and signal flares abound. The New Zealand officer relates the scene to his experiences in East Timor, Malaysia, and Bosnia. The Green Beret has, of course, seen many equally ancient cities in various war zones. "How about you?" they ask me.

This was my first tour, so I replied, "Well ... does Tijuana count?"

Chow is cooked by some local Afghans. Large delicious bread in the shape of a tire peeled off a truck, potato fries, and shish-kabob. The meat is incredibly delicious. (Not sure what type of meat). It's a great meal and I receive fair warning that I will get sick.

Time to go. One guy needs to go in the back of the pick-up and it's my turn. I put my bullet-proof vest on and lock and load my assault rifle again. We drive back into the hustle. Now that I'm on the outside of the vehicle I'm much more concerned with the fact that there are Afghans everywhere around me and almost all of them are staring at me. I scan the rooftops for possible RPG launch sites. (Although a machine gun alone could do the job on us). A Green Beret was shot in the face on this street a week ago.

The pucker factor is particularly high when the vehicle slows or stops. People crowd in and a stationary target is much easier to hit. If we get ambushed, I'll try to locate the first thing shooting at us and put lead down range for suppression until the guys inside can pick up the rate of fire and locate enemy in other directions. I've got a grenade saved for that rooftop with two or three gunmen. We speed through the town honking and dodging bad drivers. Everything is so packed that an Afghan on a moped could practically grab my weapon from where he is. A boot to the chest is the plan for that contingency. Out of the corner of my eye I see a relatively clean Caucasian standing in a dimly lit window on the second floor of a building. He gives me a thumbs up as we drive by as though he knew we were coming. Eerie.

We roll out to the suburbs with weapons at the ready, as the sun begins to set. Soon we're out where there are only the odd group of camels and the occasional adobe building. The mountains reassert themselves as the ruler of this desert and the ages that have come and gone through here. High in the sky a C17 Cargo plane silently arcs away from us and soon we're approaching the fortified American airfield. The sky on the horizon turns purple. Spread along the road here and there are dusty Afghans on their knees praying to the Southwest as they've done here for over 1,000 years.

I get a couple hours of sleep on my cot before going back on shift. I need to monitor the German infiltration and the Danish movements tonight. Also, I need to get the New Zealand officer a straight answer from Headquarters regarding some issues that came out of the meeting with the CIA agent and the Green Berets. Goodnight Kandahar.

17 AFGHANISTAN: RIDE OF THE NIGHT STALKERS

The 160th Special Operations Aviation Regiment is the preferred means of infiltration for U.S. Spec Ops Forces. If Delta Force, the Green Berets, or the Rangers need to get from point A to point B, they usually get a helicopter ride from these guys. Their number one rule is that they only fly at night. That is because it's harder to shoot helicopters down at night, it's easier to sneak the bird in behind enemy lines, and of course their customers tend to be creatures of the night as well. Thus, the 160th is dubbed "The Night Stalkers," and their chosen theme song is AC/DC's "Night Prowler."

Tonight's bird is an MH-47. The MH-47 is a specially modified version of the CH-47 Chinook cargo helicopter. The CH-47 was the work horse of the Army in Viet Nam. It hauled the big loads which Huey's couldn't handle. It's a massive beast with two rotors, and it looks more like a freighter than a helicopter. Through the 90's it was derided as an old piece of junk that had trouble staying in the air. But in the test of war in the Hindu Kush Mountains, the old battle wagon has proven its worth once again. Driving to battle in Afghanistan is tough since the road network is pathetic and the mountain passes create excellent opportunities for enemy ambush; an art which the Afghans had 10 years to practice against the Russians. So helicopter assault is the most effective way to get to the fight. But the thin air at these high altitudes hurts the ability of the helos to carry normal weight. (Imagine paddling a canoe in a lake that didn't have much water in it). To carry a normal load, therefore, you need a very large helicopter like the Chinook.

The MH-47 is the same as a CH-47 except that it comes with a CD player, chrome wheels, cruise control, and fuzzy dice on the rear view mirror. In addition it can refuel in mid-air by attaching to a refueling plane, it has extra deadly machine guns for the door gunner which spit out 2,000 bullets per minute, and most important for the Night Stalkers, is the infrared radar system which gives the pilots a near-real picture of the ground in front of the helicopter even when it's pitch black. Last, but not least, the MH-47 has a fold out jump seat in the cockpit so my lazy ass won't have to stand all night as I join the Night Stalkers on a mission.

The rotors slowly start to spin and the rumble of the engine grows from loud to deafening. Now the rotors are whipping the air down at full speed and the bird is rocking from side to side. The engine is no longer rumbling, it's screaming. The whole seen is like some Las Vegas vibrating bed gone out of control.

I can hear the pilots and crew doing their pre-flight checks. The first of two helicopters takes off without telling us, the second bird. "I wonder why they didn't radio us?" asks the first pilot. We climb to about 800 feet and start to follow the first bird. It's pitch black and I can't see a thing so I throw on my night vision goggles. Now the world is green and bright, I can see stars, mountains, and our brother bird in front of us. Instead of being two Chinooks flying in the Afghan night, we are two big fish swimming 800 feet above the floor of a great green ocean. Here and there we see a lobster driving along the floor of this surreal ocean, and the occasional colony of urchins who somehow keep their camp fires burning beneath the sea. But for the most part the bottom feeders scurry into their holes when they see the big fish coming. The big fish are here to hunt and kill.

As we glide through the valley we look to our front to find any sign of enemy activity. The door gunners cover the sides with their machine guns and for the aft of the aircraft they've lowered the exit ramp and mounted a small machine gun to fire out the back.

The mission is to infiltrate a team into a Firebase in Northwest Afghanistan. The Firebase is a small outpost of about 20 Green Berets. They've rented out a ranch house which is constructed like a desert fort. From their fort they walk or drive into the countryside looking for bad guys to kill. If they can't find any bad guys they find neutral guys, make friends with them, pay them a soldier's wage, teach them to fight, and turn them into good guys. This is an effective way to defeat guerrillas. Guerillas can hear an aircraft coming from far away, but they can't always hear a man sneaking up on them. And if you can recruit locals to assist you in the dirty job of ground combat, why not?

"Generator failure, we've got a problem!" says the crew chief over the radio.

"Well that explains why bird #1 didn't radio us on take-off, the commo' equipment runs off the generator," replies the pilot.

"Altimeter is down!" yells the crew chief, with some fear in his voice. He then went through a list of 3 or 4 other things which were "down".

"How bad is it?" asked the pilot.

The crew chief replied, "We need to turn around now, we might not make it!"

The pilots turned the bird around and headed back to Kandahar. The ride back was noticeably less smooth, but I was impressed by the calmness with which the whole crew handled this potentially dangerous situation. More impressive was that when we landed, they didn't quit while they were ahead to go have a good man-cry. We immediately jumped into a spare aircraft and got ready to go out again. Within minutes we were in the air and back on the warpath. Bird #1 had noticed that we were missing and had turned around and followed us back so we were linked up again.

Back to the long swim; a mountain here, a river valley there. Afghanistan slides under us and it's difficult to convince myself that it's real. The length of the flight is reflected by the subject of the conversation between the pilot and the co-pilot. It started out focused on technical flight details, but it soon turned to kids, wives, and golf. "Yeah hopefully we'll be back in time to catch the end of the kid's summer vacation."

"Doubt it."

"You tried that new golf course off post?"

"Oh yeah, it's great. I'm thinking about taking the wife out to it when I get back."

"It's the least you could do considering she never sees you."

"Ouch, that hurt."

"There's the strobe!" The Green Berets had put out an infrared strobe to show us where the landing zone (LZ) was. It could be seen by our night vision goggles but not by the naked eye. Bird #1 headed for it. As the bird moved in to land, an incredible amount of dust was kicked up and the bird disappeared into a brown cloud. "They're dusting out, let's pull back a bit," said the co-pilot. Soon bird #1 emerged from the dust cloud and reported that it couldn't land the bird in that dust bowl. We orbited around a bit and bird #1 looked for another place to set down. Sets of lights started popping up in the surrounding village.

"Guess we're waking up the kids," said the pilot. Bird #1 kept looking unsuccessfully for an LZ. As time passed, a series of cars started moving around on the ground. It's unusual for a small village in Afghanistan to have this many vehicles. We radioed the Firebase and asked them if they knew anything about a lot of local vehicles. They said no, and gave us a friendly reminder that Toyota pick-ups are the mainstay of transportation for third-world rocket-laden guerrillas. The vehicle movement continued to grow but finally bird #1 found its mark and landed. The team got off the bird, and the bird took off.

Given the vehicle movement, they decided to cancel our landing, and when bird #1 was up again we said farewell to the Green Berets and headed back towards Kandahar.

The ride home was on a different route. In addition to better scenery, using a different route keeps the enemy guessing in case they have any anti-helicopter weapons handy. There were a few more large mountains on this route.

In the distance, I could see the lights of our home, Kandahar Airfield. The great Soviet Air Base of the 80's was littered with the skeletons of Russian helicopters and jets. Alongside the deceased stretched an armada of shiny new American helicopters hoping to avoid the same fate which Ivan suffered 15 years back. We landed safely, the rotors wound down, and the Night Stalkers were done until the next sunset.

18 AFGHANISTAN: RADIO FREE AFGHANISTAN

Damn it! The one TV channel we get here isn't showing the World Cup Quarterfinals match between England and Brazil. It can almost be said that this soccer match will decide the cup itself! Worse yet, our American channel isn't even showing the game between Deutschland and the good ol' U.S. of A. Fortunately, our German friends have invited us to watch it on their TV which has a direct satellite link to Berlin. Ja Wohl! Foosball auf Deutsch! But the short term problem is how to follow the England-Brazil match.

Sergeant Klein noted my anger and offered a solution. Maybe his short wave radio could pick up the BBC which might have the game. He scrolled through the stations and found the BBC but it was news. No soccer game, but they had a half time update: England 1 : Brazil 1! Underdog England had actually been winning for a while early in the game. I continued to scroll around radios stations looking for the game with no luck. But although the shortwave radio didn't do much for my sports side, it had the unexpected effect of making me frightfully aware of my current location on the globe.

Have you ever driven inland from Los Angeles or New York City towards Middle America? As you leave the city you're rolling down the 8 lane freeway listening to your favorite FM radio stations. After a while the 8 lane freeway becomes a 4 lane highway and your stations begin to fade. "Dude! We're losing KLOS!" You stop for gas and while waiting in line to pay you notice a best of the 80's CD on sale for $6.99. It's tempting but you pass. Now you've got a full tank of gas, a 44-ounce Coca-Cola, and you're "On the Road Again," as Willie Nelson would say.

And it's Willie and his country crooning friends who will dominate your radio world as you continue to drive inland. On one station, the devil is going down to Georgia. On another station, Hank Williams, Jr. reaffirms that "A Country Boy Can Survive". On a third station, David Allen Coe's long hair just can't cover up his red neck. There seems to be no escape. Right about now you wish you'd invested that $6.99. Finally, you find some talk radio: "...and the Lord Jesus said unto them, repent ye sinners!"

You're feeling sorry for yourself, but you decide to try and enjoy the cultural experience. If you listen to them long enough, some of these country tunes can be catchy. Soon you're in a truck stop where a large-breasted smiling waitress winks at you, says "Hi, honey!" and brings out a 16-ounce steak with a 75-cent beer. Middle America's all right, and the radio lets you know you're there.

Well, the same radio effect occurred today in Afghanistan, a land-locked country surrounded by a bizarre mix of difficult to spell nations with radically different cultures. This was the spread of radio stations by frequency:

Frequency 16.580: Talk radio. Sounds like Farsi. Based on the tempo and inflections of the speaker's voice, my guess is that we're listening to political commentary broadcast by Radio Tehran.

Frequency 17.450: Music. The same kind you might hear in an Indian Restaurant while chowing down on Chicken Tikka Masala.

Frequency 17.685: Music. Definitely Arabian style. It's got a good beat, and you can dance to it!

Frequency 18.330: Nihau. Xie xie. Long duck dong. (Or something like that). Chinese! We're really only a stone's throw from Western China.

Frequency 18.735: More talk radio, this time from the subcontinent somewhere. Sounds like Hindi but I really can't tell.

Frequency 15.430: More Farsi ranting and raving. I guess they're in to that.

Frequency 14.320: This one sounds familiar. Russkie! Perhaps it is coming from one of our neighbors to the North like Uzbekistan or Kyrgyzstan. They had the benefit of being "improved" by Russia for many decades and speak that language well as a result.

Frequency 16.650: Stevie Wonder sings "I Just Called to Say I Love You."

Frequency 17.790: The BBC speaks about the woes of illegal immigrants coming to Europe from North Africa.

Frequency 19.220: Still more Farsi. This one seems to be an old Joseph Goebbels re-run translated to Farsi.

Frequency 20.330: Speaking of Germans, here we have a Deutsch channel; "Das Wetter ist sehr schön." Good weather, yes. It's dry and sunny in Kandahar, with a high of 115 degrees Fahrenheit.

Frequency 21.200: Here is some language which I can't even take a guess at. As you climb Northeast up the Hindu Kush Mountains the people and their languages get weirder and weirder. Perhaps this is Tajiki, or even Mongolian.

Frequency 22.350: "And the Lord Jesus said unto them, repent ye sinners!" (Didn't we leave this guy on our American road trip?)

Throw in about 6 more stations of Pashtu or Arabic talk shows, and 2 or 3 of music from those regions, and you have the Afghan shortwave radio spread, a unique blend which clearly reminds you that you're not in Kansas anymore.

Perhaps, as happened in Middle America, the music and chatter of Central Asia will sound catchy to me if I listen to it long enough. But in most of these countries, a 16 ounce steak is used to feed a village of 30, the 75 cent beers don't exist, and the large-breasted waitresses are covered head to toe with burqas.

I still haven't found out who won the England-Brazil game, but the U.S.-Germany game is about to start so it's time to go.

EPILOUGUE:

Brazil 2 : England 1

Germany 1: USA 0. USA was robbed of a second half goal by a German handball!

19 BOLIVIA: THE HEAVY METAL MILKSHAKE TOUR OF BOLIVIA

To get to Bolivia I had to fly via Mexico City and Lima, Peru. I landed in Mexico City at about 5 a.m., and I had seven hours to kill until my next flight. I was very excited to start my journey into Latin America, so I decided to make the best use of the seven hours. I found a taxi driver named Juan, and negotiated an excursion to the giant, mysterious pyramids outside of Mexico City.

Juan was 100% Mexican, but he had a long beard and wore a cylindrical white hat which made him look Middle Eastern. He said his friends all called him Taliban, and he hates it when they do that.

We walked over to his cab, and a friend of his who worked at the airport asked Juan for a ride to the bus station. Juan said it was on the way, asked me if it was ok, and I said "No hay problema."

When we dropped the guy off at the bus station he said, "Muchas gracias, Taliban," and Juan glared at him as he got out of the cab.

We drove through the north half of Mexico City towards the pyramids. Mexico City has giant lower-middle class suburbs that seem to sprawl out of the city with no end. It was too early for rush hour so traffic wasn't bad. We made it to the pyramids at about 7 a.m. The pyramids weren't due to open until 8 a.m. so we were stuck at the gate. Juan approached the gate guard and managed to talk the guard into making an exception and letting us in early since I had a plane to catch. The two large pyramids are flanked by a number of other large buildings including temples, catacombs, and various platforms, so you feel like you are actually in an ancient city.

A morning mist hung over the whole city, and because it was before opening hours, I was the only tourist in the whole complex. The pyramids, in the mist and lonely silence, took on a majestic and intimidating appearance.

Juan spoke English and gave me a fantastic tour of the place demonstrating his deep knowledge of the history of the pyramids, the civilizations which followed, and archeologists' hypotheses about the use of various buildings. Many mysteries remained unsolved. Were the pyramids used for virgin sacrifices? Were the outlying buildings public offices, markets, or houses for high priests? And above all, who actually built them and lived here? No, it was not the Aztecs. The Aztecs, who we consider ancient, did not know who built the pyramids and they looked at the city from the same baffled perspective as us. One theory says that the Nahua people built the city in 100 BC; and it grew to be one of the largest cities in the world by 500 AD, with about 200,000 people. However, Juan cautioned me not to get too comfortable with that theory because in truth, it could have been the Otomi or Totonac people, and nobody really knows.

After a strenuous and invigorating series of climbs up and down the pyramids, I paused at the top of one and soaked in the mysterious, quiet, ancient atmosphere. It was fantastic luck to be able to see this site with no other tourists. Even the ancient Nahua, if indeed that's who they were, probably never saw their city in such a tranquil, eerie light, since it would have been crawling with people when it was populated. Juan sensed that I was in deep thought mode and appreciating the awe inspiring spectacle. Unlike a typical tour guide, he knew it was time to be quiet for a while and he too sat and absorbed the moment.

On the way back to the airport, Juan pulled over by a cart that was selling fresh squeezed orange juice. He bought a large OJ for me which came in a plastic zip lock bag. You unzip the bag, put a straw in and drink. It was fresh and delicious.

We pulled into the airport and another taxi driver shouted, "Hola, Taliban!" I paid Juan, tipped him big, and complimented his skill as a historian.

On the flight from Mexico to Lima, Peru, I sat next to an American couple from North Carolina. They were going to hike into Machu Picchu, the ancient city of The Incas. Back in North Carolina, the girl was an accountant at a zoo, and the guy was an elephant trainer. We had a great conversation and after the plane landed they joined me for a 3 a.m. bowl of Peruvian soup. I caught a couple hours of sleep on the airport floor, and woke up with about four hours to kill before the flight to Bolivia. At sunrise, I found a cabbie and negotiated a three-hour flat fee for a tour of Lima. He showed me some interesting spots where revolutions had occurred, the downtown core with its impressive, old Spanish architecture, and Mira Flores, a rich neighborhood by the sea that was crawling with armed security guards.

Mira Flores had tall, modern, stylish apartment buildings and was built on a cliff which cascaded into the waves of the Pacific Ocean.

This was all very interesting, but I was curious to get a glimpse of the lifestyles of a typical citizen of Lima. "Show me where the factory workers and taxi drivers live," I said. We drove through some middle class neighborhoods that had rustic, concrete apartment buildings. Then I told the driver to go through the industrial zone and to show me Lima's poorest neighborhood. We drove back past the airport, and through a swath of ocean ports and sea containers, then miles beyond this was a massive refinery that absorbed the horizon. The driver said that over the ridge beyond the refinery was where the poor people lived. "Let's go," I said. By the time we reached the ridge we must have been many miles from the airport and a long journey away from Mira Flores. The area leading up to the ridge was empty and I hadn't seen a humanoid dwelling since the airport, only industrial wasteland.

Then as we crested the ridge, I saw a large valley spread before us teeming with what looked like a few hundred thousand people's worth of impoverished ramshackle homes, outdoor markets, and dust. It's location behind the ridge almost seemed to be an intentional urban plan to hide the scruff away from Central Lima. I rolled down my window as we drove through throngs of barefoot kids, micro-buses, goats, fish markets, and burning trash.

I breathed in deeply and confirmed that this area of Lima had an overpowering case of T.W.A. "Third World Aroma" is the phrase I use to describe the combined scents of grilled meats, rotting garbage, open sewers, camp fires, live animals, and exhaust from old cars, trucks, rickshaws, and mopeds. T.W.A. smells the same in Peru, India, Nigeria, Iraq, Western China and everywhere else on our planet where impoverished, desperate people, are colliding with the dangers and opportunities of the industrialized world. Sailors get all emotional when they smell salty, sea air for the first time in a long while; and when I smell T.W.A., I am overcome with memories of the struggles and passions of the infinite billions of poor people I have seen strung out by fate across the globe. (I also get a bit nauseated, because T.W.A. can be nasty!)

"Wow" I said to the driver.

And the driver said, "This isn't the poor area yet." We drove through the city in the valley which I mistakenly thought was the worst of Lima, and then through a stretch of tall crops which blocked the view in either direction. After driving a few miles through this agrarian tunnel, we came to the bottom of a mountain. This mountain was covered as far as the eye can see by shanties and huts made from corrugated aluminum, plastic sheets, and cinder blocks. Some of the houses were made from old shipping containers. In shanty towns around the world, a shipping container home is a luxurious status symbol since they are watertight, and you can lock them.

The driver wound up the hill, and explained to me that the government had wiped clean the side of the mountain and created this planned community in response to the massive numbers of people from the rural areas of Peru who were converging on Lima in search of work. He said they had at least brought them some electricity and were now trying to provide other basic services as well. The people in this region were so poor that for them to be able to move to the city in the valley would be a dream come true.

What shocked me most about this place was that it was not merely a poor neighborhood or district, it was an entire mountainside. The driver saw me staring overwhelmed at the sea of shanties and said, "Another Lima." Then we turned back towards the airport and he remarked that this was the first time he had ever taken a passenger to this part of Lima. I paid the driver the agreed fare plus a massive bonus since it was probably risky for him to drive to the places we had been, and he had executed the unconventional assignment without complaint. I checked in with the airline, boarded my plane, and flew to Bolivia.

Finding the right bus is normally a challenge when you are travelling in a country where you don't speak the language. But in Bolivia it's remarkably easy and efficient. I was in the central bus station of Bolivia's capital, La Paz, trying to find a bus to the city of Cochabamba. A 10 year old girl near the entrance yelled, "Santa Cruz, Santa Cruz, Santa Cruz!" almost like she was singing her favorite song. An old man slowly said "Potosi, Potosi, Potosi." Then he paused and he seemed to almost fall asleep. Then he repeated, "Potosi, Potosi, Potosi." And for almost every city in Bolivia there was someone yelling or singing its name. I heard a different 10-year old girl sing in a high pitched voice, "Cochabamba, Cochabamba, Cochabamba!"

I asked her, "Cochabamba?"

She replied, "Oh Señor!" grabbed my arm and started pulling me somewhere. She was practically running and it was difficult to keep up with her. Every few seconds she turned back to look at me and reassuringly said, "Cochabamba!" She pulled me through the bust station and up to the counter of a private bus operator. She looked at the man behind the counter, pointed at me and said, "Cochabamba!"

The man explained to me, in Spanish, that unfortunately the normal bus was sold out. He could sell me a luxury bus seat but it would be very expensive, $2.60 to be exact. I sighed to acknowledge the bad news, and bought one ticket. The bus left within five minutes, and soon we were climbing slowly out of the giant, mountain gorge which cradles the city of La Paz.

At a staggering altitude of 13 thousand feet, La Paz has one of the most unique urban geographies in the world. The central business district and the wealthy residential areas are at the bottom of a steep valley. The middle class neighborhoods crawl up the sides of the valley and spill over the top onto an endless desert-like plain. After rising up out of the valley, the bus drove through El Alto, the massive and flat suburb adjacent to La Paz where huge numbers of poor people live in a sea of brown-orange adobe dwellings. My "luxury bus" was virtually empty until we stopped in El Alto. There, a family of nine boarded, as well as a number of teenage boys carrying large sacks of potatoes. One sat next to me and packed a sack in the overhead compartment, one on his lap, one by his feet, and one by my feet. So I was virtually walled into my seat by potatoes. But no matter, because the scenery on the 6-hour voyage between La Paz and Cochabamba is a stunning display of desert moonscapes, country roads winding through bald hills, and small adobe villages.

Once in Cochabamba, I checked into my hotel which was a small, dirty, but friendly place, and only cost $7 per noche. I had a huge post-bus-ride appetite so I dropped my bags and immediately set out to hunt for food.

I had psychologically prepared myself for the possibility that during my time in Bolivia, 100% of the music I heard would be Latin rhythms such as salsa, merengue, reggaeton, etc. I enjoy this sort of music and it's always fun to make pathetic, gringolicious attempts at dancing spicy style with fine Latinas. But it is possible to suffer from Hyper-Latin-Syndrome when you listen to 2 or 3 thousand Latin songs in a row, and your brain starts to crave <u>anything</u> that sounds a little bit different. I once contracted Hyper-Latin-Syndrome on a trip to Mexico and was reduced to making a juke box play a string of Neil Diamond hits since it was the only non-Latin music I could find.

But I was in for a surprise. The first café I walked into was blaring AC/DC's "Shook Me All Night Long," one of the greatest hard rock, romantic ballads of all time. A group of Bolivian girls were dancing to this song (which was never meant to be danced to) while their boyfriends sat at the bar drinking milkshakes. Yes, milkshakes. I opened the menu and, not understanding Spanish, decided to order the first entrée on the list because I liked the spirit of its name, "pique macho." A waiter came by to take my order and said, "Ahhhhh, pique macho. Bueno." For my drink I pointed to the milkshakes those guys were drinking and the waiter said, "Liquado?"

"Si," I replied, and he showed me a section on the menu which had 11 or 12 different liquados, all for incredibly cheap prices: Chocolate ice cream blended with bananas and milk; strawberries, guava, and milk; papaya, peach ice cream and milk; and many more. As a dairy-o-holic, I was in paradise.

After I ordered, Mettalica's "Battery" came on the juke box. This is a classic heavy metal tune which evokes emotions such as "smash everything into little pieces" or "mindlessly trudge towards an evil objective." It was fitting background music for a game which several men in the café were playing called, Gacho. Gacho is an intense Bolivian dice game which involves shaking the dice in a cup and slamming them on the table as hard as you can, then glaring at your opponent in the eye before examining your dice and marking your score.

My liquado arrived. I had gone with a conservative approach and ordered the chocolate ice cream with bananas and milk option. I sipped this delicious mix to the tune of Van Halen's "Runnin' With the Devil," another bang-your-head rock song which somehow the Bolivian girls had found a way to dance to.

Enter the pique macho: As the name implies, pique macho is man-food. Imagine a 4-story building, (and the dish seems to be a about that big). On the first floor, there is a mass of greasy, fried potatoes, possibly imported by the teenager who sat next to me on the bus. On the second floor are thick chunks of grilled beef. On the third floor there is another layer of fried potatoes, just to give the building extra strength. The fourth floor is where the hot dogs live, and the roof of the building is made of tiles of melted cheddar cheese and onions.

I used my fork like a wrecking ball and started to demolish the gastronomic edifice. As I bulldozed through the sausage and potatoes, I started to fill up, but I was rallied by the sound of heavy metal Gods, Black Sabbath, singing the song "War Pigs." After pigging out on the grilled beef and the extra layer of potatoes, I was met with an unpleasant surprise: in addition to the 4-stories on the top of the pique macho, there was also a basement of boiled eggs and still more cheese and potatoes.

I was bloated but dug through and made it to the bottom as Motley Crue sang the triumphant "Home Sweet Home." I sat inert for about ten minutes digesting, reveling in my achievement of consumption. The Scorpions came on to the Juke Box to sing "Winds of Change" and I took this as my cue to ask for the check and change bars.

I figured I had found the one heavy metal bar in South America, but after walking a few blocks I popped into another café and ordered a liquado with Papaya, ice cream, and milk. Again, the music was hard core heavy metal, and again there was a collection of men playing Gacho, and tattoo-free girls on the dance floor. I chatted with the owner, a woman named Lina whose giant Labrador dog sat at the bar with her. She said she had a degree in food science from Florida State University and had used it to develop a new hangover curing drink called, "El Buen Dia." Even though I wasn't hung-over I sampled this all-natural fruit concoction after finishing my liquado. It was an invigorating beverage.

Lina introduced me to an exotic woman who was waiting to give a tango class. The music slowly transitioned from heavy metal to Pink Floyd to Tango. The tango instructor glided over to the dance floor and proceeded to teach two Bolivians how to tango.

I transitioned to the next bar and on the walk over I noticed herds of stray dogs and a cluster of 12-year old boys staggering up the street who Lina had said were "the glue sniffers." Bolivia has a massive orphan problem, and many end up literally living in sewers and surviving on petty theft and shoe shining. Later in my stay, I visited an orphanage with some do-gooders and repaired broken beds and cabinets. The orphans were ecstatic to have visitors and many cried when we left. Donations to help these kids are complicated since there are numerous corrupt, bureaucratic layers of waste in between foreign money and the orphans. The best way to donate would be to blaze through Bolivia on a bad-ass Harley motorcycle and each day visit a new orphanage, play with the kids, talk to the director about what things they need, and then go shopping with them the next day to buy an ATM withdrawal's worth of products they can use such as bunk beds, food, clothes, kitchen equipment, etc.

My next liquado was a vanilla ice cream, pineapple, and milk special at a Reggaeton bar. Reggaeton, not to be confused with Reggae, is a harsh, energetic mix of Latin-style salsa-rap. I danced with a couple of Peruvian girls who were in Bolivia for medical school. They were very fun and they attempted to teach me some near-impossible Peruvian dance steps. One of the girls had downed a few too many mojitos, and she started such a ruckus that security kicked her out. She was actually so drunk that she couldn't walk, and her friend asked me to carry her out of the bar into a taxi. Then at the taxi she begged me to come with them because she lived on the 2nd floor of her building and wouldn't be able to get the drunken one up the stairs. So I escorted them home, and carried the now sleeping girl up the stairs and onto her bed.

Then the sober girl took me to her room to show me a big poster of 50 children from an orphanage in Peru where she used to volunteer. She gave me a 20-minute monologue in Spanish about their situation (which I didn't understand). I heard words like "pobrecitos" (poor babies), "solitario" (lonely), and "hambriento" (hungry), and tears started to come to her eyes. After this she made me listen to her favorite reggaeton music, and introduced me to her cat, Señor Lucas. We said goodnight after making plans to go to her favorite restaurant later in the week. (Burger King). On my way out the door she said, "Gracias," pulled my hand and gave me a long, passionate French-kiss.

The night was still young so I walked towards a salsa club which Lina had recommended. I was on a street crowded with old women dressed in the traditional indigenous Bolivian style. This consists of giant hoop dresses and 1920's bowler hats. The use of this costume was originally forced on indigenous women by the Colonial Spaniards, but now it is seen as a symbol of indigenous pride, and the way a woman wears the hat can indicate her marital status and desires. If you are standing still when they walk past you, their skirts are so big and rigid, and they move so slowly, that it feels like a battle ship is cruising by.

I couldn't find the salsa bar, but I found a sidewalk café which was 100% dedicated to liquid chocolate. I stopped for a cup of molten chocolate with a dollop of mint sauce. A woman of about 67 overheard my poor attempt to order in Spanish, and she asked if I spoke English. "Nelly" had lived in Bolivia, Brazil, Europe, and America for 30 years. She spoke five languages and she was the tragic lover of an Argentinian cattle tycoon who was married, but in love with Nelly. She was with two old Brazilian businessmen who she was teaching English to. They used the chance to practice new English words on me, and they gave me a good description of life as owner of a rubber plantation.

Nelly made me try a different style of liquid chocolate, a spiced variety that came with almond shavings, and when the bill came they wouldn't let me pay for anything. After the chocolate place, Nelly insisted I come with them to a bar called Whiskeria in the lobby of the 5-Star Grand Hotel Cochabamba. At this bar I signed up for "The Grand Liquado" a house specialty with a variety of fruits and ice cream. We met another Brazilian who claimed to be a millionaire, then an Irishman who claimed to be a billionaire, and then an Australian girl who claimed to be flat broke and travelling around the world. She gave me her business card which simply said, "Vagabond."

Nelly's brother used to be The Governor of Cochabamba and there was a continuous stream of people at the bar coming to say hi to her. A fantastic pianist played "Don't Cry for Me Argentina," and other haunting, nostalgic South American classics. Nelly then introduced me to another friend of hers who turned out to be the exotic tango dancer from Lina's bar. Later, Nelly caught me eyeballing a very sexy cocktail waitress, and since she knew all the staff at the hotel she introduced me to her as well. Before leaving Whiskeria, I had amassed contact information for a sizeable number of interesting people to meet later in my trip.

Nelly also taught Spanish, and I decided to hire her. I took lessons from her twice a week in her luxury penthouse apartment. Her rate was $5 per hour, and this included a fantastic spread of gourmet dishes she would make such as prosciutto, French cheese, various Bolivian appetizers, and Colombian coffee. She usually reeked of alcohol during the lesson, and after class she would give me about an hour long lecture on Bolivian politics, and the melancholy drama of her relationship with the Argentine. Her income came partly from subsidies from her lover, and partly from U.S. social security. At the end of my trip, I hooked her up with a few more customers, other Americans I had met while in Bolivia.

The Whiskeria started to close down so I asked the bartender for directions to the salsa bar. After saying goodbye to the Grand Hotel crowd, I walked towards the salsa bar and en-route, I stopped for some meat-on-a-stick snacks sold from a cart by a woman wearing the bowler hat outfit.

The salsa bar was packed, smoky, and all the Bolivians I met there said, "Oh, this isn't real salsa; you have to go to Colombia or Cuba for that. And the real merengue is in Brazil, and the real tango is in Argentina." But to my uneducated eye, all of these Bolivians seemed to be experts at the Bolivian versions of all these dances.

I ordered a mint, banana, chocolate chip, and milk liquado, and started talking to a French girl who was even worse at salsa than I. She was with a polyglot group of Bolivians and Europeans. One of their people was a Bolivian guy named Alvaro. Alvaro said he was an award-winning film director, for his documentary about life in Bolivia. But as he put it, "No one ever watches my movie, and I lost a lot of money making it. But, it gets me laid." Then he said, "Hey, see this girl in the purple sweater over there with her boyfriend. She can't stop looking at me. Every 20 seconds she looks at me. Watch … 3, 2, 1…" and right on cue the girl looked at Alvaro, and smiled. Then Alvaro said, "Ok, this is crazy but … wish me luck." He had a hoodie which he pulled up so you couldn't see his face. Then he walked over to the girl in the purple sweater and started flirting with her. She pulled and tugged at his hoodie laughing and eventually pulled it down. (Thankfully, the guy she was with turned out not to be her boyfriend).

As the salsa bar closed, Alvaro organized his entourage into taxis and invited me to come with them to his apartment for the after-party. The after-party was cool. The French fille was there, along with about 20 other people. One guy was from a rare Bolivian indigenous tribe, and he looked exactly like the oompa-loompas who work in Willy Wonka's chocolate factory. I talked to this guy for a while about life in Cochabamba. He said the biggest recent drama here was a great fire in "La Cancha." La Cancha is a giant bazaar selling clothes, kitchenware, maize, tires, and all the things you usually see in a developing world market. The fire, apparently, ripped through La Cancha in the middle of the night wiping out 30% of the retail space, destroying millions of Bolivianos worth of merchandise, and killing 1 poor dog. I heard the story of the La Cancha fire many times over the next week. And it's a testament to the friendly Bolivian character that every time someone told the story, they told it as if the retail space and the merchandise were no big deal, but the loss of the poor dog was tragic.

A couple hours later, Alvaro was on the couch making out with the girl in the purple sweater, while most of the guests did tequila shots. Around sunrise, I took a taxi back to my hotel. There was a bar next door so I decided to go in for a liquado night cap.

This last bar was called "Passage," and it had what looked like Asian Kublai Khan decorations on the outside so I wasn't sure what to expect. It was seven or eight in the morning so, not surprisingly, there were only about five people in the bar; including one couple and three Bolivian head bangers.

As it turned out, the pan-Asian decorations (which also ran through the bar's interior) had nothing to do with the music, drinks, or food. The music was 100% heavy metal, the drinks were either cheap beer or liquados, and the food was pique macho.

The head bangers started talking to me and I asked them what their favorite heavy metal song was. They all said Mettalica, "Seek and Destroy," and the bartender played this song twice in a row. One of the head bangers was about 5' 4", and had long, metallic hair down to his waist. He said, "Wait, watch this…" and he played air guitar while banging his head and lashing the bar with his hair from two feet away. "Isn't that cool?" he asked.

I finished the night with another big, pique macho, and a raspberry-vanilla liquado. I said, "Hasta la vista head bangers!" to the guys at the bar, and went back to my dive hotel to sleep.

20 INDIA: THE SIEGE OF JAIPUR!

Most great journeys involve a truck stop. This is especially true in mysterious, chaotic India. For only 125 Rupees (about $3) you can get an eight hour bus ride involving near death collisions, surreal scenes of the Indian countryside, and at least one break at a truck stop. The truck stop's restaurant is a row of dirty shanties serving up fresh grub from the neighboring village. If you can ignore the flies and the close proximity of the restroom, (i.e., group of unfortunate trees), the food is actually delicious.

I savored fresh tomatoes and cilantro on a bed of Naan bread while admiring the freight capacity of the heads of the village women. Clad in immaculate, brilliantly colored saris, these women can haul the equivalent of an American pallet load. As I wondered who hauls the heavier cargoes, a caravan of eight camels sauntered past the truck stop, each carrying at least half a truck's worth of crops. And how do they move a full truck load? Later that day the bus got stuck in traffic behind a truck-size bundle of straw being carted by … an elephant!

But the challenges of transporting goods around the Ganges were of minor importance compared to the real task of the week: **The Siege of Jaipur!** The desert kingdom of Rajasthan centers on the sprawling city of Jaipur. Jaipur, in turn, is protected by a series of 3 mighty mountain forts. If you capture the forts, you can capture Jaipur. If you capture Jaipur, you can seize Rajasthan. My goal was to test the defenses by hiking up to the top of the mountain, through the 3 forts, along the route an invader would have to take.

A glance at the map showed it would be a long, uphill trek and I began to have second thoughts since I was still recovering from a violent illness. "Perhaps I should spend the day at the hotel bar drinking gin and tonics, watching Youvraj Singh take wickets for the Indian cricket team?"

But then there was a sign: the four lane highway next to the truck stop which was normally packed with speeding, horn-honking maniacs, suddenly cleared. For a solid, eerie, minute there were no cars, trucks, or even camels. Then a holy man appeared on a white horse! He looked me right in the eye, and gave me a wave which only a man on a spiritual journey could give. It was crystal clear at that point; the siege must go on!

My bus started to honk its horn and rev its engine. It was time to get back on. It occurred to me that a holy man on horseback on the Indian interstate was probably less out of place than Greg Holt, of 33 Sleeper St., Boston, USA being on a public bus in rural Uttar Pradesh. I jumped on the crowded bus and fortunately Nimriss, of mud hut #16, Mathura, India, had saved my seat. Like most Indians I met outside of Delhi and Agra, Nimriss spoke no English, but was very friendly and managed to communicate with me anyway. At one of the stops where the hawkers board the bus, he bought me a samosa (golf ball of tasty food). Later, I bought him some chai (tea in a clay cup) and tossed a coin to a beggar who was missing a few limbs.

The bus picked up momentum and we headed for Rajasthan. Indi-pop blared from the bus speakers and a gang of teenage girls sang along. It sounded like my favorite song from the wedding I had just been to, so I tried to join in: "Azhee-Baji… Azhee-Baji, Azhee-Baji, Waji, Waji!" Nimriss clapped his hands while a farmer and his wife tried to control their seven kids.

Things got livelier when we stopped at a hovel of a town in the middle of the night and six surly villains out of a Bollywood film got on the bus. They had just come from a shack that had a large ad saying "Thunderbolt!!! Strong Beer!!!" These liquored-up passengers passed the time by throwing random debris out the window at unsuspecting targets. They yelled at each other constantly, and kept everyone else awake for about an hour. Then they all passed out in unison.

This left me in peace to gaze at the small towns passing outside the window. The main streets of these towns were a series of concrete or mud cubes which served as store fronts by day and homes by night. Families gathered together around small fires and every nook and cranny in the web of buildings housed a sleeping human, bull, or pariah dog. One town had a larger cube which had a band and a big festive dance going on. It made me homesick for the fantastic wedding of the prior week. Those were my decadent Delhi days with India's educated elite; never ending feasts, urban high rollers, and beautiful women.

The next morning I was in Jaipur ready for the assault. I caught the 5 Rupee bus to the Fort of Amber. The first line of defense of any Indian fort is the throng of guys trying to sell you postcards or take you to their uncle's shop. I wound up in uncle's shop and bought some jewelry for my cousins.

Once past these aggressive gate keepers, I made my way up the slope. The fort was truly imposing and I could see no way to access it, other than right up the main road which was entirely watched by parapets. (So an attacking enemy would be carved up by gunfire even before getting to the entrance.) Once at the fort, I was met by the second echelon of defenders, the tour guides. I hired a guide, and his tour was excellent. It was the equivalent of having a private tour with a professional museum docent, and well worth 150 Rupees.

Amber Fort doubled as a harem, so while the exterior was designed to trick the enemy into attacking in the wrong direction, the interior was designed to trick the occupants into not knowing which room the king was in. As the tour guide put it, "All of our kings were very sexy men!"

I spent an hour wandering around the confusing halls and chambers, and wound up at the CD shop which was tended by a teenager in a jean jacket.

"Namaste", I said.

"Namaste," he replied.

"Good tunes."

"Thank you, sir."

"I'm looking for that song that goes, "Azhee-Baji… Azhee-Baji, Azhee-Baji, Waji, Waji." He looked at me like I was crazy. Then I sang it again more slowly and his eyes lit up. He scrambled among some open CD's.

"I think you mean this one, sir." He popped in a CD and I recognized the familiar tune. The song built up strongly to the chorus of "Kazhee-Raw-Ray, Kazhee-Raw-Ray, … Kazhee-Raw-Ray, Raw-Ray, Raw-Ray." (Not quite Azhee-Baji, but close enough!) I was excited to find the song, and immediately bought the CD for less than the price of the tour guide.

With Kazhee-Raw-Ray in my head as a battle anthem, I started up the hill again towards Jai Garh Fort. As you round the first corner, it's obvious that anyone attacking Amber Fort would be under continuous fire from Jai Garh Fort. So it would be near impossible to take Amber without first taking Jai Garh. But to take Jai Garh from this direction would require walking right past the fortified guns of Amber (equals a quick death). Therein lay the genius of this castle. (Well … that and the mirrors on the harem ceilings.)

The battle raged just beneath the gates of Jai Garh Fort. This time the defenders weren't touts or tour guides. Rather, they were the fine fighters of the elite Rajasthan Monkey Regiment. A few centuries ago, this fort was defended by 22,000 men. There now seem to be that number of monkeys guarding the place. The king of the monkeys sat aloof on top of the fort, considering his next move and observing the enemy's attack in the valley. His troops did battle against a boy armed with a sharp stick. The boy looked scared, but an Auntie-Jig (older woman) behind him spurred him on. Already, the monkeys had managed to steal two wreaths of flowers from the Auntie-Jig's altar and she wanted the boy to fend them off.

Once the walls of Jai Garh are finally breached, the attacker is rewarded with a magnificent view of Amber Fort below. At the top of the fort, you can see an old cannon which would have lobbed shells into the valley. In the background, you can barely see a more modern type of fort: large radar towers on the ridgeline keeping a watchful eye on Pakistan to the Northwest. (As a side note, if you ever fly north from Delhi at night you will see the amazing spectacle of blotches of light marking the sea of cities and towns which virtually cover North India. Suddenly there is a solid, bright, twisting line which stretches as far as the eye can see. This is the defended border between India and Pakistan. North of that is the densely lit Indus valley population center. Then the mountains of Afghanistan rise up and all the lights go out…)

"Did you find peace in India?" asked a student in the fort's café.

"No," I replied, "I'm a nomad. I move around too much for peace."

"You should try Yoga," he said. I had a great conversation with two college students while I munched on onions and pekora. The business student talked about investment opportunities in India, and the geography student explained how rain dries up so quickly in Rajasthan that there is no river which drains it. Their family sat in the background but didn't speak. (Although the mother burst out laughing when I described the Indian suit I wore to the wedding.) I showed them my new CD and they pointed to the guy on the front and said, "That's Bunti and Bubli. He's Big B's son! We love Kazhee-Raw-Ray!" Apparently Big B is a famous Bollywood star and now his son is in the business.

The road to the last fort, Nahargarh, looked flat for a change. I started to walk it and within a kilometer came upon a milestone (in the old fashioned tombstone by the road-side style) that said "5." Bad sign. My feet were already blistering from a new pair of Indian shoes and I was weary from the long hike to the top of Jai Garh. I thought perhaps the "5" was just there to confuse attackers, and pressed on. I kept a pace count, and sure enough, as my count reached 1 kilometer there was a milestone saying "4," so I had four kilometers to go. Worse, the "flat" road was actually a series of ups and downs crossing the ridge line.

The sun was getting low and I estimated that it would be about setting by the time I reached the top of Nahargarh. Then I would either have to fetch a ride, or walk back the five kilometers in the dark to Jai Garh, then another eight km to the main road where I could catch a rickshaw. It was a bad idea, but with the holy man urging me on and a sense of fatalism which I'd been using in India, I decided to continue. It would all work itself out somehow.

Along the ridge there was the occasional goat herd, and one or two groups of stick collectors. These groups consisted of a man using a stick with a V on the end breaking branches off of trees, and two women collecting them on their heads. Fire wood must be scarce in the valley for them to walk so high up. I wanted to take their picture, but decided it's best not to piss off a guy who snaps limbs for a living.

I was pretty exhausted when I reached milestone "1". A moped pulled up next to me. It was the two students from the café. They gave me a ride for the last kilometer (three to a moped is standard in India) and the whole ride everyone was singing "Kazhee-Raw-Ray, Kazhee-Raw-Ray, … Kazhee-Raw-Ray, Raw-Ray, Raw-Ray."

The view of Jaipur was worth whatever transportation troubles awaited me. The walls of the fort hide the sights and sounds of the city below, but as I reached a gap in the wall I suddenly heard the overwhelming din of an Indian city. In one place you could see super modern office buildings, probably housing genius Indian Institute of Technology graduates designing the next cell phone. In another place you could see packs of dirty kids flying kites or chasing goats. Paved roads with the occasional Mercedes adjoined mud paths with bulls pulling carts. One neighborhood's homes were almost all painted blue, signifying that the owners were Brahmins. Another neighborhood was a muddy slope crisscrossed by ditches and ramshackle huts with tin roofs held down by bricks. It was the natural drainage point for the city, and the roads were covered with the vile run off of an ad hoc sewer system. The visual experience was reinforced by the confusing sounds of horns honking, children yelling, old machine shops hammering metal into useful shapes, animals barking, mooing, chirping … (plus a few more animal noises).

To study the layout, I picked a random spot in the view with my finger and tried to trace a path to the center of the city, or even a main road; impossible. I've decided that urban planning in India is as follows: Where there is a vacant lot, a high tech startup company will emerge. If there is no high tech company, a shop selling vegetables, jewelry or rugs will appear. In the absence of a shop, a shanty town grows. And if the shanty dwellers don't want the vacant lot, a cricket game will break out.

I climbed on top of one of the higher parapets, and settled in for the sunset. The cricket games began to shut down, (disappointing one angry young batsman), the shops closed up, and the traffic tapered off. Then a slow tranquil voice came over the whole city singing some enchanting prayer. It may have been the call to prayer for Jaipur's Muslims, I wasn't sure. Whatever it was, it was great background music for an Indian sunset on a mountain. If my student friends were here I could now report that at least for a few minutes, I had found peace. I had not used yoga, but with the long walk ahead of me the stretching probably would have been a good idea.

There was only one group of tourists left and they were four to a rickshaw, so I didn't dare ask for a ride. Since tourists normally don't walk up to Nahargarh, it made sense that for once there were no cabbies or touts hustling for a fare. Darkness fell and the place was pretty much deserted except for a few families huddled around fires living in some of the fort's ruins. This was one of those traveling low points where you're tired, hungry, thirsty, and really just want to beam yourself up to the Hotel Enterprise and call it a day. Unfortunately, that wasn't an option.

But alas! These are the moments which demonstrate the greatness of traveling alone! Only the solo traveler can do something obscenely stupid, get into a terrible mess, find a way out, and enjoy the whole experience. This could have been a time for "Whose idea was this, anyway?", "What were you thinking?", "Next time we're going to Florida!" Endless arguments over how to resolve the situation, forced promises to never do this again, intermittent whining, the occasional outburst of tears, constant reminders about how much someone's feet hurt etc. Nay, the individual traveler can see it for what it is: a golden opportunity to see the lights of Jaipur on a moonlit night! A refreshing evening stroll! A chance to hear the sounds of India's night creatures in the woods! Yes, I was truly blessed. The ridgeline I was on had the dramatic specter of Jaipur's lights on three sides, and ahead were my forts, now brightly lit up. In the valley to the right was a serene lake with a palace floating in the middle. Before I knew it I had paced off several kilometers. My night vision was razor sharp, my feet stopped complaining, and I still had half a bottle of water left.

This ridgeline at night took on a totally different character. It reminded me of Mullholland Drive in Los Angeles. It was a beautiful rambling drive with hundreds of spots where people could pull over, watch the view and escape the city. Sure enough, I began to see cars parked on the side of the road, and could hear people talking about 40 feet off to the side.

I finally reached the "5" milestone again. It was still another eight kilometers to the main road, but it was all downhill. After a couple kilometers downhill, the steep mountain stole the moonlight. The woods seemed to grow thicker and in the pitch blackness my imagination had a chance to create all the things you don't want to run into in the woods. I couldn't help recall something from my guide book: There's some special religious significance attached to cobra snakes. As a result, some parts of India are crawling with cobras. I had to ask myself the same question which Indiana Jones asks in Raiders of the Lost Ark: "Snakes?! Why did it have to be snakes?" Why couldn't it be sacred squirrels? So of course, every twisty branch now looked like a cobra to me and every critter noise I heard was a slither. Just as I started to run through scenarios in my head of how I would hop down the mountain if a cobra bit me, a car came barreling down the hill and screeched to a halt. Two guys offered me a ride to the bottom of the mountain, and I jumped in before they had a chance to change their mind.

Ashu and Sanjay were suburban family men who'd been given a free pass from their wives for a guy's night out. Their wives checked in on them with cell phones about every ten minutes, but they were still allowed to drink beer and smoke. They were one of the cars I had passed on the ridgeline and it was clear that they'd been pounding Kingfisher beer and yapping about old school days. It was pretty much what you'd expect from two old friends on Mullholland Drive.

After seeing what sober driving in India was like, I didn't like the idea of drunken Sanjay trying to steer his way downhill. On the other hand, I was extremely relieved to not have to walk down the rest of that serpentine road. Ashu spoke just a little English, and told me about his jewelry business and the percentages of which stones come from India versus South Africa or Japan. Sanjay didn't speak English but he was able to demonstrate that it's ok to urinate pretty much anywhere in the city, even if you're in full view of a busy street.

These two were really cool and offered to drive me all the way to my hotel even though it was way outside the city. This would save me the hassle of getting a rickshaw, and I was having fun telling jokes with these guys in Hindi-English-Sign-Language. I dropped an "Ap ka naam kya hai" on them and they were very impressed. That means "what is your name?" and of all the things my friend Sumit taught me to say in Hindi, this sentence by far got me the most free food, useful tips, photo ops, and general good will.

Ashu and Sanjay described how they never go to bars and rarely to restaurants, but have loads of fun arranging parties with the families of their friends. Everyone comes over and they cook, eat, dance, and sing. A guy's night out like this is at best an annual event. That's probably a good thing based on the number of near miss accidents we had. In one case, Sanjay swung the wheel to the left and took us half way off the road. A beer bottle on the car floor hit me in the foot and through the cigarette smoke which filled the car I saw a full grown tree coming out of the middle of the highway. So while I thought Sanjay was driving us to our death, he was actually just getting into the slow lane, which happens to be to the left of the tree, while the fast lane was to the right. The tree was like an aggressive version of a speed bump.

Down the road we pulled over for yet another piss break. But this time there was something else afoot. What I thought was a road side shack was actually the neighborhood liquor store. I got out of the car to take care of business then walked over to the counter with Ashu. "What kind of beer do you like?" he asked.

"Kingfisher."

"Good choice," he replied, "Do you like Strong Beer or Laser Beer?" What the hell was Laser Beer?! I thought it might be India's equivalent of the North American Ice Beer fad. Basically instead of fermenting the hops, the beer companies iced it over or something and marketed it as a new breed of beer. Was Laser Beer where they zapped the hops with a supercharged beam for extra flavor? I didn't like the sound of Laser Beer, but then I flashed back to the midnight drunks on the bus ride who had been drinking Thunderbolt! Strong Beer! I didn't want to end up like them, so Strong Beer was out. By now a crowd of the local drunks had gathered in curiosity, (not too many tourists stop off here), and the impatient liquor store owner was shoving away an inebriated old buzzard who was trying to snatch a bottle of the Indian Army's favorite rum, Old Monk. "Do you like Strong Beer or Laser Beer?!" repeated Ashu.

I shook my fist in the air and yelled, "I'll take a Laser Beer!" Ashu cheered, handed over the Rupees, and the owner uncapped a gigantic, frosty, Kingfisher beer that said "Lager Beer" on it.

So we set off on the road again, each with 600 ml of lager in hand. Sanjay's wife called and for a while he was using one hand for the phone, one hand to drink his beer, and a knee cap for the steering wheel. It sounded like he was in trouble so Ashu took the phone and said in English, "Just a little more time. We're with our new friend from America." Once he hung up I showed them my CD. I proudly said, "This is my new CD. These guys are great, man, Kazhee-Raw-Ray rocks. Oh, and that's Big B's son."

Ashu said, "Wow. This is a great CD. You know your stuff, buddy!" Ashu then called Sanjay's wife again and said, "This guy is so cool! He knows who Big B is!"

I saw my hotel in the distance. I knew I was home free, and could celebrate my triumph. Soon I would be on American Airlines Flight 293: 40,000 feet above the saris, salesmen, sugar cane and spices. I knew I would miss this strange land where families treat you like one of their own, teenagers care about the state of your enlightenment, and most people understand the principles of physics. I had achieved **The Siege of Jaipur!** I had walked a total of about 20 steep kilometers. I had discovered that yoga is the secret to peace. And I had polished off an oversized Laser Beer. There was only one thing left to do, and my friends Ashu and Sanjay clapped their hands, stomped their feet and joined in singing: "Kazhee-Raw-Ray, Kazhee-Raw-Ray, … Kazhee-Raw-Ray, Raw-Ray, Raw-Ray!"

ABOUT THE AUTHOR

Gregory D.B. Holt has been a construction worker, a fish gut scooper, a pool lifeguard, a business consultant, an American soldier, and a travelling philosopher. He has earned degrees from MIT, Pepperdine University, and West Point. He is currently conducting research for his next book in the proletariat neighborhoods of a Ukrainian industrial steel town.